WHY WALKING

WITH GOD IS NECESSARY

FOR LOVE, HAPPINESS, PEACE, & JUSTICE.

WHY WALKING

WITH GOD IS NECESSARY

FOR LOVE, HAPPINESS, PEACE, & JUSTICE.

Lorenza James

Studio of Books LLC
5900 Balcones Drive Suite 100
Austin, Texas 78731
www.studioofbooks.org
Hotline: (254) 800-1183

Ordering Information:
Special discounts are available on quantity purchases by corporations, associations, and others. For details, contact the publisher at the address above.

Printed in the United States of America.

ISBN-13: Softcover   978-1-964148-46-5
           eBook   978-1-964148-47-2

Library of Congress Control Number: 2024909936

ACKNOWLEDGEMENTS

I would like to dedicate this book to all my family members, friends, well-wishers, and those who encouraged me and allowed me to share their journeys through the stories of their lives. First and foremost, to my immediate family whom I love dearly and pray constantly for them. My wife Deborah has given so much of herself during our 50 years of marriage to ensure my success. I am thankful for her love, support, and encouragement. God blessed us with five children who I treasure with the highest appreciation: Lorenza James II (Atom), Michael, Rachael, Amy, and Matthew. I am blessed of God to have them as our children. I value each of them for who they are, their persons and personalities. I am equally grateful for our eight grandchildren: Lorenza James III (Trey), KeiAmber, Michael II, MaKenna, Alexis, Matthew II (MB), Zoe, and Paxton; one great granddaughter, Nirobi (Anna). These golden nuggets have been a joy to our family. I am thankful to have in the family Jeremiah Brown (Amy), an outstanding son-in-law. Special thanks are extended to Tabernacle Missionary Baptist Church and the members I have been blessed for 28 years to serve as their pastor. Additional thanks are extended to the many people, some are depicted in this book, who allowed me to share and present their walk of faith with God. I appreciate you all.

Table Contents

INTRODUCTION

Walking with God is the process of moving in a renewed spiritual relationship. The avenue by which you gain access to possessing the peace, love, and happiness that most people seek for their lives. I say most people because, unfortunately, there are some people that have endured such difficult behaviors, or tragic events, or abusive relations, and/or negative living, that they have adapted themselves to bitterness, hatred, and rejections of regular, or spiritual relationships. For many in such a mindset, they would rather console themselves in apathy. The ability to walk with God begins with a new spiritual life which comes in the process of being born again. Being born-again does not prevent anyone from experiencing personal hurts, pains, or rejections that come through human relations. What it does is give you the comforting understanding that God will keep you through it as you trust Him to provide better. Life is too important to regret, too real to lose, and too beautiful to ignore. Surrendering your life, or emotions to negative conclusions, or negative attitudes only takes away joy from your life. Daily walking with God is a spiritual fellowship that need encircled faith to trust, growth to live, and praise to worship.

Being born again is the spiritual process that provides renewed persons changed minds, changed hearts, and changed perspectives. It also instills within each person's life, or walk with God, the desire to live so that others will recognize God's presence in his/her life. Walking with God is a life of personal willingness. Willing to hear God's Word, willing to accept His love, and willing to live for Him. This acceptance of the spiritual life releases the believer from the bondage of sin. Jesus spoke of this spiritual freedom and deliverance offered to all that walk with Him. He said, "The Spirit of the Lord is upon me, because he hath anointed me to preach the gospel to the poor, he hath sent me to heal the brokenhearted, to preach deliverance to the captives, and recovering of sight to the blind, to set at liberty them that are bruised," (Luke 4:18-19, KJV). Hearing and receiving this message of love, provide believers this committed personal relationship with God.

The focused interest, of walking with God, is emphasized spiritual living, and lifestyles that followers of Jesus Christ need to portray. Christians' lifestyles often influence unbelievers' views of God, and the church. It also reflects, and impacts the respect they may have for Christians. That is why Christians must, at all times, live in, and out of their faith. This will avoid even the appearances of unacceptable behaviors that erode their character, their integrity, their image, and their church. Some people are always watching Christians to find fault with them, and/or their behaviors. These fault-finders exist at every junction, avenue, street corner, and back alley. Their main agenda is to prove that the church is filled with nothing but hypocrites. Perhaps these "fault-seekers," through their agendas, are motivated by some bad experiences with the church or church members. Or perhaps they feel that somehow God had let them down. Regardless, many of such thoughts, have concluded that they don't need the church to be Christians. It is true you don't have to go to church to be a Christian. Not all church members are Christians. Yes! There are hypocrites in churches. However, others' behaviors should not prevent your recognition of church importance and participation. The Bible tells us that Christians need to come together, share fellowship, strengthen one another. "Not forsaking the assembling of ourselves together, as the manner of some is; but exhorting one another: and so much the more, as you see the day approaching," (Hebrews 10:25, KJV).

There is a distinct difference between being a Christian, and being a church member. The same can be said of the differences between church memberships, and spiritual relationships. A church member is someone who has joined the church. A Christian is a person born into the Body of Christ. However, when it comes to church membership. A person can have a long-serving church membership record without ever experiencing spiritual renewal. You may question, how could that be? Simply stated, Church memberships involve the process of joining. The procedures for joining a church are usually based on the church's denominational doctrine and criteria for receiving members into its organization. Such requirements often include having the person(s) make a public statement desiring to join, and agreements to abide by, or conform to, the creed, doctrines, and religious practices of the desired church, group, or denomination.

Christians are more than church members. They are members of the Body of Christ, as well as having memberships in the local church. However, when it comes to the spiritual relationship with God, it becomes more about personal examination of the heart. The message from Paul to the Jews in Rome, "That if thou shalt confess with thy mouth the Lord Jesus, and shalt believe in thine heart that God hath raised Him from the dead, thou shalt be saved," (Romans 10:9, KJV). No person, without being born again can enter into this spiritual relationship with God. The honest confession of the need of a saving Christ in his/her life. As a new creation in Christ his/her spirit is renewed. "Therefore, if any man be in Christ, he is a new creature: old things are passed away; behold all things are become new," (II Corinthians 5:17, KJV). Church members are often led to believe that the two are the same. They rest their spiritual confirmation on congregational approval.

The reason Jesus is the hope of salvation is that God has given Him a name above all names. "Neither is there salvation in any other: for there is none other name under heaven given among men, whereby we must be saved," (Acts 4:12, KJV). The spiritual process of being born again gives new life, and provides renewed personal relationship with God. Christians' lifestyles must be seen as trying to serve both God, and the world. Jesus said, "No man can serve two masters: for either he will hate one, and love the other; or else he will hold to the one, and despise the other. You cannot serve God and mammon," (Matthew 6:24, KJV).

A Christian is a person born again by the Spirit of God, and recognized as having surrendered his/her life to the service of God. "For ye are bought with a price: therefore, glorify God in your body, and in your spirit, which are God's," (I Corinthians 6:20, KJV). The Christian walk is a journey based solely on who we are in Christ Jesus. If we are to walk with Jesus, we must spend time with Him, trust Him, and obey Him. "Can two walk together, except they be agreed?" (Amos

3:3, KJV). Therefore, conflicts come when the Christian walk is measured by our steps, rather than Christ's footprints. "And he saith unto them, Follow me, and I will make you fishers of men," (Matthew 4:19, KJV).

Therefore, church people with this mindset lack the spiritual ability to influence unbelievers to accept the Christian faith, virtues, and values. Perhaps what's most unfortunate about the lack of influence is that church members sometimes blame non-church people for not being interested in the church. Instead, they should consider their inability to influence others. The power to spiritually influence unbelievers rest on Jesus' proclamation that Christians' lights must shine so that men may see their good works, and glorify the Father in heaven (Matthew 5:16). Instead of being the light that Jesus intended, the church, at times, seems to be in spiritual darkness as well. This darkness is not lost darkness, but spiritual ignorance darkness. Now before you think that I am being rude, crude, or self-righteous because I used the word ignorance, please allow me to emphasize what I am saying. I grew up cringing and going on defense whenever I heard someone refer to me, or others as being ignorant. Thinking it was a negative reference, or a put down. Perhaps the person speaking at the time may have meant it to be so. However, ignorance simply refers to something not known, or understood.

The strength to overcome ignorance is knowledge. Spiritual knowledge improves awareness of man's need of a right relationship with God. It seems, at times, that church folks are satisfied with having the basic understanding of God. This acceptance limits Christians' spiritual hunger for growth, knowledge, and desire to walk with God. Without spiritual growth, Christians become less motivated, and not spiritually equipped to live for God. Therefore, if the joy of the Lord is to be the believers' strength, then they must allow their spiritual relationship to awaken within them the desire to love God, serve God, and to walk with God, (Nehemiah 8:10, KJV).

Church talk is the way Christians converse with each other through a language that's saturated with well-spoken words which sound holy, and righteous, but yield hollowness. Words that include, love, kindness, happiness, and joy. Unfortunately, many church members receive poor grades for how these elements are practiced, or displayed. Therefore, if Christians are to experience the true calling of sinners into the sainthood of Christ, these words must be spiritually rooted in their hearts, and activities. They must reflect the embodiment of the spiritual life, with Christ being the center of all that is done. Christians must maintain the hunger for righteousness, (Matthew 5:6, KJV). It must motivate the love for God in believers' hearts, and direct services performed in His name.

The church is God's city set on a hill that cannot be hidden. Jesus told the church to "Let your light so shine before men, that they may see your good works, and glorify your Father which is in heaven," (Matthew 5:16, KJV). The church must again reflect the spiritual interest of Christ. As His ambassadors, go into the highways, and hedges to invite the "Whosoever will" to come out of darkness into the marvelous light, (Luke 14:23, I Peter 2:9).

Walking with God, in the Christian life, is to be more than good sounding slogans. It must represent Christians' spiritual relationship, and personal growth in Christ. Walking with God is embracing the ministry life of Jesus which began at the Jordan River. He was baptized by John the Baptist (Luke3:21-

22). Afterwards, He spent 40 days in prayer, meditation, and fasting (Matthew 4:1-2). When it was time for Him to choose men to walk with Him, ordinary men were selected. These men had no special religious skills, or educational training in religion that distinguished them from any other men around them. What made them chosen men was their willing spirit, and cooperative attitudes. These traits were what Jesus used to teach, and trained them to walk with God.

Jesus' earthly ministry focused on touching lives, saving souls, and preparing men to build the Kingdom of God on earth. His personal attention was given to these ordinary that He prepared to be witnesses of Him "Both in Jerusalem, and in all Judea, and in Samaria, and unto the uttermost part of the earth," (Acts 1:8, KJV). His spiritual walk was the example they needed to walk with God. It is important to note that the places He went to recruit these men were not the Jewish temples, the Jewish synagogues, or the religious schools. These willing followers of Jesus were not trained to attain religious titles or positions in the religious orders. Rather, these men of Jesus were found working on fishing boats, and sitting at tax collecting tables, as well as other common occupational works. When Jesus called them from their tasks by asking them to follow Him (Mark 1:17, KJV), they responded immediately. They dropped what they were doing, and followed Him. His invitational words captured their attention. They chose to do His work.

During the ministry years of Jesus, the church was established, and defined. He told His disciples, "Upon this rock I will build my church …," (Matthew 16:18-19, KJV). The purposeful impact of the church was/is to serve as shelters of restoration for all seeking refuge from an uncaring world system. This vile system, of relentless selfishness, destroys promises, and turn spiritual dreams into nightmares. Therefore, it is necessary for church members to be seen as one Body in Christ, heard to be the voice of God calling sinners out of darkness, and shining as God's marvelous lights of hope. This message of love must go out to the hurting, discouraged, damaged, hopeless, and lost people. They must know there is room for them in the house, and family of God. The purpose and meaning they are seeking will be found in their needed spiritual relationship with God. Walking with God is necessary for worship, love, peace, happiness, and justice.

"Why Church Matters"

In January 2020, a virus was identified in China as the Coronavirus. A plague that later would immobilize the world. At first, it appeared to have been an issue that only the Chinese government, and its people had to contend with. That concept, or thought was short-lived as the Coronavirus soon went from being an epidemic of enormous proportion, in this eastern nation, to being a pandemic that crippled the entire world systems. It's contagious outpour on the world caused millions of people to die. Here, in America, the President of the United States, along with states governors, and local leaders sought to protect the public. Together, they prevented the spread of this virus with mandated restrictions in public gatherings. These limitations required businesses, public accommodations, and all large events, and gatherings of people, including churches, to modify their activities for health and safety reasons. These measures were the best available efforts to prevent the spread and destruction of this pandemic. It was believed, by most, that these restrictions would cause the virus to be of short duration, but more than two years later, the pandemic remained a costly health issue not fully resolved. The virus infected more people than initially imagined, with a greater number of Americans dying than many believed was necessary. Fortunately, great progress has been made to subdue, and eradicate the strength of this virus through appropriate vaccines developed through the medical research of dedicated scientists, and medical technicians.

The Coronavirus pandemic caused the whole world to stop, for a moment. Activities were halted or cancelled, for a while. Movements by citizens were slowed, cautiously. Work and schools became virtual implementations of productivity, and learning. They were displayed from home rather than the office, or in the classroom. Likewise, the church had to make similar adjustments. Sunday worship services no longer had the assembly of melodious singing choirs, or worshippers filling the pews. Caution and precautions became the established means, and methods. Facebook became a useful medium for conducting worship services to avoid spreading the virus, or people becoming contaminated. With safety at the core of all church activities, minimum numbers of members attended in-person worship services, with majority of members worshipping remotely. This soon became both a positive, and a negative for members considering the return to in-person church worship. On the positive side, most churches have not suffered financially during this pandemic. In fact, many churches finances increased. It appears that more people committed to worship through Facebook than attending church before the pandemic.

The other side of this coin is the negative impact of in-person worship. Many church leaders, clergy and laity, agreed that adjustments made during the pandemic may cause church membership to decline. A significant number of previously committed members may not return to in-person worship. Some members willing to support the church financially may prefer to continue doing it from their homes rather than returning to in-person worship. This pandemic provided, for some, an ideal religious situation; going to church without leaving home. It would be like having your cake and eating it too.

As more people become vaccinated, and immune to the Coronavirus, church members are encouraged to return to in-person worship. However, it appears that a great number of church members are content paying their monies without attending in-person services. The following questions demand responses: Does church still matter? Is it a spiritual necessity? Can people's spiritual needs be met without going to church? Will the church cease to be an important social institution? Well, in spite of these, or similar questions' doubts about the church relevance, the ultimate answer has already been made by the One with the authority to speak. "Upon this rock I will build my church, and the gates of hell will not prevail against it," (Matthew 16:18, KJV). Perhaps the parable, in Matthew 22:1-14, where Jesus talked about a man who made a great supper and invited certain people to attend, best describe the attitudes and contentment of some church-goers after the pandemic. Just as these three men who initially agreed to come, and later changed their minds, some church members may have second thoughts about church attendance.

In the parable, the father had much preparation done to get ready for this event to honor his son. He greatly anticipated the invited guests' arrival. However, when it was time for the event, one after the other made excuses not to come. One said that he had purchased some land. He had to go inspect it. He asked to be excused. Another one said that he had bought five yokes of oxen. He needed to prove them. He asked to be excused. The third one said that he had married a wife. He could not come. He too asked to be excused. Being disappointed with their responses, the father commanded his servants to go out into the highways and hedges and invite others to the celebration.

Church matters. Its influences in the world are life changing. Its appeal attracts the lost, the hurt, and the brokenhearted. Church members, in their roles as shining lights, must go into the darkness, and lead whosoever into the marvelous light of God. Church matters. Its significance must never be reduced to being about any one person, or groups of peoples' feelings, opinions, or comfort. It must remain a sacred place that gives reverence to the glory of God. After the pandemic, church members' enthusiasm for in-person church worship should be akin to how David, king of Israel, felt when he was finally able to return to the house of God. "I was glad when they said unto me, let us go into the house of the Lord," (Psalm 122:1, KJV).

WHY WALKING WITH GOD IS NECESSARY FOR WORSHIP

PART I

CHAPTER 1

Getting Ready to Worship

"We have come into His house, gathered in His name to worship Him. So, forget about yourself and concentrate on Him and worship Him. Let us lift up holy hands and magnify His name, and worship Him. Worship Him. Jesus Christ the Lord." This 1997 contemporary praise and worship song by the Maranatha Singers inspires my spirit to commune with God in worship. Worship is the spiritual practices of Christians' devotion to Jehovah God. There are many styles, and methods to worship services ranging from ultra-conservative, where little to no-noise is permitted, or heard in services, to the highly emotional, and boisterous services that invite all the noises your spirit will allow you to give. There are no right, or wrong procedures for worship. The qualifying involvement is that whatever form of worship participated, that it be true, heart-developed, and spirit-fulfilled. Let it be real. The question of how, and where worship takes place is a topic that sometimes becomes confrontational discussions among religious people. Thank God, the true answer is not lodged in religions. Jesus, one day, had such conversation with a Samaritan woman at Jacob's well.

According to her religious teachings, she believed that worship occurred only in selected places. Specifically, in the Mountains of the Lord. However, Jesus explained to her that true worship was not about places, or creeds, or any defined locations. True worship is spiritual. "But the hour cometh, and now is, when the true worshippers shall worship the Father in spirit and in truth: for the Father seeketh such to worship him. God is a spirit: and they that worship him must worship him in spirit and in truth," (John 4:23-24, KJV).

The Lord, our God is Holy. He is worthy to be praised. It is true. God is worthy to be praised. The spiritual desires of Christians are to praise God through worship services. The elements of worship are normally applied to our praises confirming our spiritual connections with Go. These elements include fervent prayers, upbeat singing of songs, and dramatic preaching. Although well intended, these acts of worship, at times, becomes nothing more than ceremonial activities. Going through the motions of worship often leave many Christians, in church services, searching for spiritual validity. To appear spiritual in worship, some Christians fake their praises to impress others. This approach to worship leads to misunderstanding the purpose of worship. Worship was never intended to be about the worshipers. It is about the one being worshipped. It's about God. When the focus of worship is on how well worshippers perform, it becomes false worship. True worship is to God. God alone! The spiritual connections between God, and man stirs up the longing in the spirits for Christians to glorifies God in praises. Spiritual worship, and praises to God require worship leaders to set the tone, and create the atmosphere for worship through songs that lift up the name of Jesus. When spiritual leaders, through their worship experiences, lift the spirits of congregations to levels of praise where worship is realized, then thanks are given, and worship is achieved.

Creating a wonderful worship atmosphere can be a difficult process to accomplish when the spiritual concepts for worship is inhibited by church doctrines, dogma, and litanies that often lack ability to motivate congregations to praise God. Without the spiritual energy to "feel" the presence of the Lord, church services become dull, repetitive, and lacking spiritual fire. Most Christians are sincere in their efforts to worship God. Their desire, and motivation for praise is for more spiritual power, for better understanding of worship, and for real worship to occur.

Jesus was a true worshipper. During His three-years ministry, He is recorded to have worshipped only a few times in synagogues. He was notably found on numerous occasions worshipping God in prayer and praise. Such occurrences include: His baptism. He spent 40 days worshipping in the wilderness (Matthew 4:1-2). After His feeding of 5000 men, beside women and children, and having sent His disciples away, He privately worshipped and prayed (Matthew 14:23). When He knew His time was near, He went to the Garden of Gethsemane to worship and Pray (Matthew 26:39). There were many other times, and occasions Jesus spent time in worship, and prayer without attending services in the synagogues. As He told the woman at the well in Samaria, worshipping God is not limited to the specified locations. Worship with God can take place anywhere, at any time because "God is a Spirit: and they that worship him must worship him in spirit and in truth," (John 4:24, KJV). Through busy schedules, long days of ministry works, tired body, and all other reasons to delay, or put aside worship, Jesus made time. He knew the value of worship. It is renewal strength. It is redeeming power. It is ability to reignite passion. Energy to do the Lord's work, Jesus made time for worship.

Worship is giving praise to God. David, king of Israel, musician, and renowned Psalmist penned these inspirational words of praise. "Praise ye the Lord. Praise God in his sanctuary: praise him in the firmament of his power. Praise him for his mighty acts: praise him according to his excellent greatness. Praise him with the sound of the trumpet: praise him with the psaltery and harp. Praise him with the timbrel and dance: praise him with stringed instruments and organs. Praise him upon the cymbals: praise him upon the high-sounding cymbals. Let everything that hath breath praise the Lord. Praise ye the Lord," (Psalm 150, KJV).

CHAPTER 2

Church Worship

S unday morning worship services, in Christian churches, provide a variety of worship expressions to the glory of God. The aim and goal of church gatherings are to worship God. A popular saying, that's often repeated needs a spiritual adjustment. Instead of saying that Christians are to "Enter to serve, Depart to worship," as some acclaim. Should note, more spiritually accurate, the phrase be reversed. The understanding should be that Christians enter the church to worship, and after worship has taken place, they depart to serve. A simple rearrangement, and the order for coming in and going out of the church will determine the effectiveness of worship services. Although worship services vary in churches based on church litanies, or order of services, there remain the common agreement that God must be the center focus of worship. Otherwise, worship becomes nothing more than what the Apostle Paul described as one "become as sounding brass, or a tinkling cymbal," (I Corinthians 13:1b, KJV); just making noise. Church worship must be more sacred to church activities than just doing something, or just doing anything to stir up emotions justifying religious services.

The church is precious to God. He will not tolerate it to be toyed with, denigrated, or taken for granted. Jesus, during His last week on earth, after riding into Jerusalem on a donkey, went into the temple and cast out the moneychangers, turning over their tables. He declared before them all the importance of the church. "It is written, My house shall be called the house of prayer; but you have made it a den of thieves," (Matthew 21:13, KJV). There were seven churches in Asia Minor that Jesus singled out, comparatively, as to what is required to keep the temple of the Lord sacred, spiritually focused, doctrinally sound, and full of caring compassion. These churches represented types of spiritual leadership, and worship of God. They reflected the power of spiritual influences on members, and communities to exalt the name of Jesus in worship. The seven churches identified were: Ephesus, Smyrna, Pergamos, Thyatira, Sardis, Philadelphia, and Laodicea, (Revelation 1:11b).

The church at Ephesus (Revelation 2:1-4) was known to be an orthodox church. Members of this congregation were considered to be those who practiced traditional views of church, and religion. It was identified by Jesus for having done good works, having patience, practiced sound doctrine, and hated evil. These commendable traits suggested that this church was the model for ages to come. However, the one flaw, Jesus said that He found in this church revealed their misunderstanding of holiness, and the hollow practices their worship services had become. One important element of church worship, for them, was missing. That ingredient was their loss of love. They had lost their love for God, people, and the church. Therefore, their worship services no longer had stimulating power to move them through the process from worshipping God to serving God. Sad to say, the church at

Ephesus reflects churches today that are become so immersed in traditional church worship, and practices, 'the way things have always been done', that they have no room in their hearts to worship God.

Smyrna (Revelation 2:8-9) was a church with little financial resources. It was considered to have been a poor church because of it. Yet, it was heralded as being rich because of the faith, and trust they had in God. Members of this congregation practiced spiritual endurance. They practiced the principle of wealth that Jesus spoke of "Lay not up for yourselves treasures upon earth, where moth and rust doth corrupt, and where thieves break through and steal: But lay up for yourselves treasures in heaven, where neither moth nor rust doth corrupt, and where thieves do not break through nor steal: For where your treasure is, there will your heart be also," (Matthew 6:19-21, KJV). Because Smyrna's devotion to pure spiritual worship Jesus had nothing but words of commendation for them. Churches today that best emulate Smyrna's congregation are missionary focused churches enduring persecution.

The church of Pergamos (Revelation 2:12-14) and its congregation's worship of God was affected by what they accepted as being in bad surroundings. Jesus commended them for having the spiritual insight to recognize evil. Their awareness of Satan's ploys to disrupt true worship of God. However, recognition without the willingness to reduce its grasp, or influences on the church yielded complicity to the events, and activities that invaded the church. It corrupted them. They tolerated corrupt church doctrines, and teachings that did not conform to the norm. Churches that practice this form of worship are government supported entities.

The church of Thyatira (Revelation 2:18-20) was a congregation of believers whose worship, and praise of God was commended by Jesus. He noted that the church was charitable. Their worship services were highly spiritual. They emphasized among members the impact faith, and patience have on their lives. However, the shortcomings they permitted to saturate their congregation were lack of spiritual discipline, and allowing misleading teachings into their worship services. Extremely persuasive speakers infiltrated the church, and created a cult-like following which diluted their worship of the true and living God. Churches today that align with this spiritually tragic display of worship are cults masquerading as Houses of God.

The Church of Sardis (Revelation 3:1-5) was listed as a dying church because their format for conducting church activities, church discipline and doctrines, as well as their intended worship services had become unproductive. Jesus had no commendation for this church. It was for them as Jesus referenced the Christian life in the Sermon on the Mount. "Ye are the salt of the earth: but if the salt have lost his savour, wherewith shall it be salted? it is thenceforth good for nothing, but to be cast out, and trodden under foot of men." Their inability to influence church growth reduced them to decline, and the congregation to an imminent death as a worshipping body. Church growth is essential for sustaining vibrant congregations. When churches stop growing, they soon become extinct. There are churches today that wrap themselves in formalism believing that such structures will provide spiritual development. However, such churches end up dying.

The Church at Philadelphia (Revelation 3:7-11) is recorded to have been a weak, but loyal church to the doctrine of Christ. Jesus found no faults with their praise, worship, or practice. They were commended for keeping the word of God. Their faith was a strong testimony. They reflected the image that Jesus declared that the church be, "Ye are the light of the world. A city that is set on a hill cannot be hid," (Matthew 5:14, KJV). Today's churches that would partner in faith with the Church at Philadelphia are those earnestly worshipping God in spirit and in truth.

The Church of Laodicea (Revelation 3:14-19) was a compromised Church. It was classified as being lukewarm, neither hot, nor cold in its worship, and praise of God. This church had no redeeming spiritual qualities. Worship in today's churches, like that of Laodicea, would be churches concerned with being popular, self-focused congregations, and more conditioned for worldliness than spirituality.

CHAPTER 3

Worshipping The Unknown God

The Apostle Paul found himself in confrontations about worship on Mars Hill. He waited in Athens for his fellow companions, Silas and Timothy to join him there. During their missionary journey, they encountered persecution from religious groups in several cities where they preached, and taught people about Christ. Certain members of these groups falsely accused them of causing confusions among the people in the cities. Paul, and Silas were quickly and quietly ushered out of one city to the next. When they arrived at the city of Berea, false accusers followed them, and caused problems for them there. Paul was encouraged to move on while Silas, and Timothy remained in Berea with the intentions of joining him later in Athens. In Athens, Paul noticed how prominent idol worship was practiced. He disputed with the Jews worshipping in the synagogue. The evil environment didn't seem to bother them. Some philosophers mocked him. They called him a babbler. A presenter of strange gods. Because of his strong witness of faith in Jesus Christ, he was taken out to Mars Hill where people argued religion daily.

Mars Hill was a place devoted to shrines honoring gods. The people there were careful not to leave any religious representation without recognition. However, in case one or more gods were not identified, an altar was erected to the "Unknown God." Paul took advantage of this opportunity to give the unknown god, a name, an identity, and true representation. In the spaces dedicated to this population of idol gods, Paul revealed to them Jesus, the true God of worship. He challenged their knowledge, spiritual understanding of worship, and who they should be worshipping. He referred to them as been "Too superstitious," (Acts 17:22b, KJV). He made known to them that the God he worshipped was not made by human hands. Neither the worship of Him is restricted to temples. He is the Lord of heaven and earth (Acts 17:23-24). "For in him we live, and move, and have our being," (Acts 17:28a, KJV).

Paul was bold in meeting the challenges of religious clarity. He was strong in proclaiming the good news of Jesus Christ. He was encouraging for those willing to hear, and receive the spiritual truth he espoused. He was inviting to any that believed the gospel, and wanted to embrace life in Christ. However, when he spoke of the resurrection, some mocked him, but there were some there that wanted to hear more (Acts 17:29-32). Paul soon left Athens for other places. While there in Athens, he worshipped God. He praised God. He worshipped, and praised God in the temple, and on Mars Hill.

"We have come into this house, gathered in his name to worship him. We have come into his house, gathered in his name to worship him. We have come into his house gathered in his name to worship Christ the Lord. So, forget about yourself and concentrate on him and worship him. So, forget about yourself and concentrate on him and worship him. So, forget about yourself and concentrate on him and worship Christ the Lord. Worship him, Christ the Lord," (Maranatha Singers, 1997).

WALKING WITH GOD

PART II

CHAPTER 4

The Choice Between Two Roads

The Christian life is a journey of faith, belief, and spiritual assurances that as you walk with God, you are never walking alone. Being alone is an undesirable situation. Being lonely is both hurtful, and needing. Being isolated from others is a discouraging way to live, or approach life. Walk with God, and He will direct your path to a life filled with love, peace, and happiness. This spiritual walk with God is not a quick fix, or a short journey. It is a lifetime commitment. It is a spiritual process that leads all who by faith invest his/her living in spiritual growth. Through knowledge, and spiritual understanding of God's word, will achieve success in this life, and the reward of everlasting life.

The Christian life, or walking with God is about choice. When God created Adam and Eve, He placed them in the Garden of Eden. It was two significant things that God gave them that are applicable to all human beings. One was the breath of life, and the other, that of having a choice (Genesis 2:7; Genesis 3:3). In Genesis 2:9, during the creation process, God planted a tree which is called The Tree of the Knowledge of Good and Evil, in the middle of the garden of Eden. Adam and Eve, caretakers of the Garden of Eden, were told by God not to touch, or eat from that tree because they would surely die. It was about choice. Choice is the awareness, or differences that exist between one, or more things. For Adam and Eve, the choice was either believe God, and obey Him, or believe someone else, and disobey God. This choice was neither a challenge, or a temptation for them by God. However, Satan, in the form of a beautiful serpent invaded the garden. He spoke to them through enticing, tempting, and persuasive words of inquiry. He challenged their understanding, and passive obedience to God. When Satan asked why they didn't eat from this tree? Eve told him that God restricted them from the tree because they would surely die (Genesis 3:2-3). Satan countered this directive by God with one of his own. He told them that God was not being honest with them. He told them that they would not die as God said for eating off the tree, but rather their eyes would be opened. They would become wise as gods (Genesis 3:4-5). His words were so persuasive to Adam and Eve that they chose to believe the half-truths of Satan rather than the truth of God. When they chose to eat from the tree of the knowledge of good and evil, they died, as God said they would; not physically, but spiritually (Genesis 3:7-22, KJV). Their actions, and decision altered their spiritual relationship with God. It subsequently affected all human interactions, and spiritual relationship with God. Therefore, from that time forward, in human history, the relationship between man, and God was broken. The damages done through choice changed the spiritual relationship to the point now, the unholy mankind could no longer fellowship with God, who is Holy. Choice, the opportunity to choose between directions, feelings, worship, and deities must be applied with the understanding that choices bear consequences.

Perhaps there is no greater spiritual comparison concerning making right choices than that which Jesus taught about choosing between traveling two roads. One road, Jesus described as being broad and wide with many travelers on it. The other road is said to have been narrow with few travelers on it. Whereas the end of the broad road is destruction, the end of the narrow road leads to eternal life (Matthew 7:13-14, KJV). The choice people make between the two roads will determine their travel, and their life destinations. One of my all-time favorite poems, written by English poet Robert Frost, is entitled, "The Road Not Taken." In this poem, one traveler comes to a fork in the road, and must make the choice as to which road, or direction should be taken. "Two roads diverged in a yellow wood, and sorry I could not travel both." Which would be his choice? He could not travel both. The traveler reasoned and rationalized the choices. The decision made, "I took the one less traveled by, and that has made all the difference."

Walking with God is choosing the path that will make differences in your life. Jesus walked with God. In putting together His ministry team, Jesus chose fishermen named Peter, Andrew, James, and John as His foundational leaders. They were selected for several reasons, including being willing to follow Him. He didn't have to coerce their involvement. Another reason for choosing these fishermen was because their craft taught them the benefits of being patient, and persistent toward their tasks. Fishermen are competitive with nature; often battling the elements of wind, and rain to catch fish. These kinds of temperaments the fishermen possessed Jesus found useful in teaching, training, and developing them to be spiritual leaders. Jesus asked them to follow Him. He would teach them, in like manner, to catch men (Matthew 4:19,

KJV). Having learned how to maneuver through difficult situations, as well as through sunshine, and stormy weather, they came to understand that walking with God, would at times become a difficult journey.

CHAPTER 5

"Order My Steps in Your Word"

A mong the significant challenges Christian leaders, and believers, face today are ways, and effective methods that help the church to have more spiritual meaning to people. This concern is both important, and urgent. Church outreach efforts must be designed to influence people who have not made church a priority part of their lives. Therefore, the church must not stand as an idle monument to truth. Rather, confirm its role in the ministry of God, the spiritual "City set on a hill" (Matthew 5:14, KJV). Christians must not permit the church to be viewed by worldly standards. That is perceived to be nothing more than well-decorated worship places that lack the ability to influence, attract, and direct changes in people lives. The church cannot effectively carry out its spiritual responsibility by waiting for worldly applause, or worldly approval.

Walking with God through Christ Jesus is the most effective way to know Him. Knowing God fills life's emptiness. Knowing God brings spiritual happiness to all seeking fulfillment, and feelings of completion. Therefore, it is necessary for those seeking better relationships with God, to understand that walking with God is important for spiritual growth, and personal development. People lacking knowledge of God, and unfamiliar with the purpose of walking with God, are often left feeling that God is not concerned with them at all. Those harboring the perspective that God only cares about Christians are wrong in their understanding of God. People with this wrong belief often feel that the Christian life is reserved for people without problems, faults, or issues.

The misunderstanding of God's love, that He only cares for selected people. If this was true, which it is not, would be both frightening, and discouraging. The message of God through the church must be clear. God has no respect of person. All is welcomed in God's house. Holier-than-thou persons must not be the lasting images unbelievers have of the Christian life. The truth of the matter is that becoming a Christian is not a finished product. Rather, it is a developing relationship restored through faith in Jesus Christ. According to the Southern Gospel singing group, the Hemphills, "He's still working on me." Words in the song include the following: "There really ought to be a sign upon my heart, don't judge him yet, there's an unfinished part. But I'll be better just according to His plan, fashioned by the Master's loving hands. He's still working on me …"

Being a Christian is not a finished product. To apply the words of a well-used contemporary song recorded by the Gospel Music Workshop of America Women of Worship choir, "Order my steps," walking with God is a step after step process for change, growth, and development. Many people and choirs have sung this song. There is one singer that have done it as well as others. She is a dear sister named Lenora

Jones. She is a member at Weeping Mary Missionary Baptist Church, Tuscaloosa, Alabama, where Reverend Ricky J. McKinney is pastor. Whenever she sings this song, it sounds like a personal testimony of her faith, and walk with God.

Walking with God in songs. This dear sister sings to the glory of God. Her voice, filled with praises, lifts high melodious spiritual sounds. She sings as she walks with God. She sings because God is real. She sings because her love for God is true. Through faith in God, she has learned to walk through personal tragedies, struggles, and failed commitments by trusting God. Her personal tragedies that have weighed heavily on her walk with God included her family members. More specifically, tragedies involving her siblings, that I will lovingly refer to as being the "Melton Crew." The names of her sisters were Brenda, and Gloria, and their brother Theopolis. Her mother, Mrs. Leoide Ladner Melton, whom she meticulously, and lovingly cared for, as her caretaker, passed away in 1999 after being diagnosed with cancer. However, prior to that time, the Melton Crew would gather at their mother's house each Sunday afternoon to share times of love, laughter, and fond memories. Her sisters, like she, possessed musical, and vocals skills that they used in the church to praise God, and uplift the spirits of fellow-worshipers. Her sister Brenda was gifted on the piano, and organ. Her sister Gloria had the gift of song. Brother Theopolis demonstrated faithfulness in church work, and participation. These siblings, as diverse as they were in mannerism, habits, and behaviors, shared a loving bond that after the sudden, and unexpected death of each of them, Lenora found herself feeling left alone.

"Order my steps dear Lord," became more like a prayer than mere words in a song for Lenora as she said good-bye at the bedside of each of her siblings' death. Brenda, her oldest sister, was dealing with some intense legal issues involving one of her sons, along with some other family troubles when a brain aneurism cut her life short. The loss of Lenora's big sister, as she referred to Brenda, meant no longer having that special person that she could talk to about everything that mattered. This bond allowed them to give, as well as receive from each other, personal counseling about their troubles through their loving shared relationship. Although Brenda's death did not alter Lenora's faith in God, nor her walk with God, it did cause her to pause as she absorbed the pains of this loss. Brenda's death was sudden. It shook her faith a little. However, to avoid becoming negative, or depressed about her sister's death, Lenora reminded herself that Brenda, her big sister, was a woman of faith. She was a woman who walked by faith. She was a woman, regardless of the situation, would by faith trust God. She reminded herself that Brenda's faith in God believed that nothing happened to her that God would not carry her through. This faith reminder gave Lenora peace in her heart. The peace of God, because she knew that Brenda, her big sister was at peace in Christ.

"Order my steps dear Lord." Gloria was the youngest child born to her parents. Unlike Lenora, who was quiet, satisfied with staying home, and not concerned with doing too many things, Gloria was almost opposite. She was strong-willed, extremely vocal, and outgoing. She was not the kind of person that liked to stay in, or around the house all the time. For Gloria, there were places to go, people to see, and things to do. Lenora and Gloria often clashed over their contrasting lifestyles. Yet their love, and care for each other wouldn't permit, nor allow their bond to be broken. As the years passed, the sisters grew closer to each other, and their lifestyles became more similar as

Christ became the center of their living. However, for Lenora, sudden tragedy struck her again when she learned that Gloria had cancer, and was diagnosed being in the later stages of the disease. When Gloria sang in the church choir, peoples' spirits were touched. Those listening could feel the presence of the Lord in the songs. One of my favorite songs she sang was "City Called Heaven." Words in the songs included, "I am a poor pilgrim of sorrow. I'm left in this wide world alone. I've started to make Heaven my home." Gloria moved congregations with the singing of this song. Heaven was in her heart, and in her singing.

Watching her sister fade away as she sat at her bedside in Hospice, Lenora found herself in the chapel praying for her sister, and for herself. Her faith in God did not waver, but she wondered whether she was being tested by God. She wondered whether she could handle the test. Because of her quiet demeanor, and not being one that engaged in many things outside of the home, she often felt like she was the family's weakest link. To her surprise, her sister Gloria wouldn't leave her thinking that she was the weakest link. "No!" Gloria told Lenora that she was not the weakest, but rather the strongest one of them. She said that it was Lenora's faith in God that made her strong. As the hours closed on Gloria's life, Lenora was by her bedside. Looking at Gloria, she whispered to her, "You can't leave me! I need you!" Gloria, in her weaken state replied, "I know sis."

"Order my steps in your word dear Lord." Lenora's walk with the Lord had all the elements, and reasons to give up this faith-based walk with God. Her personal tragedies, and loss of loved ones had become emotionally, a difficult journey. However, Lenora's walk with God provided her the spiritual strength to trust God. Walking by faith is not always a clear path of understanding how, and why things happen to us, and those we love. On her spiritual journey, Lenora had learned to walk by faith through grief, sorrow, and death. With the loss of her mother, and youngest sister Gloria to cancer, her oldest sister Brenda to an aneurism, what else could happen? What more could she take? Well, the answer came to her in another startling phone call. This one came from her sister-in law Elizabeth telling her that her brother Theopolis had become ill, and was taken to the hospital. The diagnosis of his condition was dire. She found herself praying "Lord, don't take my brother! Don't take him." He didn't make it through his attack. After Theopolis died, she found herself asking such questions as, "Why God? Why didn't you take me? Why have you taken everyone that I loved? Why am I left alone?" Theopolis' death, as with her other siblings, came with little to no warnings. His death was a hurt words could not console. She said, "It hurt so bad."

"Order my steps in your word dear Lord, lead me, guide me every day. Send your anointing Father I pray! Order my steps in your word." Lenora continues to sing this song of praise, which for her, could partner as her prayer on this spiritual journey. Lenora is a woman who loves God. She loves to sing to the glory of God. The loss of her mother, and her siblings, at times caused her to feel like she was left alone. However, the spiritual promises of God comforted her walk. "If God be for us, who can be against us? (Romans 8:31, KJV). "He will not fail thee, nor forsake thee," (Deuteronomy 31:6, KJV). Lenora's faith allows God to continuously order her steps.

CHAPTER 6

Faith-Walking, The Examples We Set

I t is not uncommon to hear some church people speaking, or boasting about their faith in God; or their walk of faith with Him. However, I have learned that what attracts people more readily to the church, is not so much Christian talk as much as it is the sincerity they observe in Christians' walk. For people who don't go to church, whether unbelievers, or believers that have lost interest in church, they are looking at church-goers for truth, hope, love, and spiritual directions. Questions that shape their observations include: Are these people real? Do they practice what they preach? Are they fakers and pretenders? Do they just want my money? Do they really care about me? The answers they are seeking from such questions are called spiritual examples of walking with God.

The Christian church, for the most part, has been viewed in society as a place where faith, and trust in God is emphasized. Its positive image of providing hope, love, and care for people has always been its spiritual message. Those attending church have found it to be a respected place of worship. However, for many people with no church affiliations, want to know whether the church will make any differences in their lives.

Christians who love God, and church must lovingly give such inquiries reasons to come to church, engage the church, and participate in the church. This is most effectively done as Jesus directed, when church members "Let your light so shine before men, that they may see your good works, and glorify your Father which is in heaven," (Matthew 5:16, KJV).

For those unsure about the church, and its spiritual impact on people lives. Don't be misled by people without spiritual knowledge, and church discernments! The church is a strong tower of faith, belief, and trust. It is the House of God. It is a place of warmth, love, care, and of salvation. It is God's place where anybody can be considered somebody, and where nobody is more important than anybody else. There are some people that often speak ill of the church, or raise doubts about the sincerity of church members. These are usually people that have been hurt in some ways by someone at, or associated with the church. Perhaps they may have felt that in their times of need the church failed them. This hurt is called church-hurt which seems to have a more lasting pain on those involved than any other kind of hurt. Therefore, they speak negative things about church. However, before any judgements are made toward the church, or its members, take time to know them for yourself. Let your assessments be made on what you have learned about the church. Not on other peoples' determinations. The church is not a concept, or creation of man's thinking. The church belongs to God. Jesus said that, "Upon this rock I will build my church; and the gates of hell shall not prevail against it," (Matthew 16:18, KJV).

Perception of a person, place, or thing can become reality if it is not countered with truth. Truth requires honest, and fair examination of the topic, or issue. There are many people who do not have either membership, or association with any church, but have negative opinions, and perceptions of the church. There are numerous reasons why some people may think, or feel negative about the church. One is called perception. This view, or attitude about the church may not be biblically, or spiritually valid, but for these people, it is an impression conceived in their reality. They often blame church people for their resistance, rejection, and negative attitudes toward the church. For this, and other reasons, the Christian church must remain spiritually focused, physically functioned, and ready with a clear message of hope. This spiritually defined identity will eliminate many negative perceptions of the church's meaning, purpose, and operations.

The Christian church remains the magnet of hope for those seeking spiritual relationships with God. That is why Christians must constantly seek to attract people to receive Christ as Savior. Christians are to be spiritually sensitive as to how they relate to people through what they say, how they say it, and in what tone, or colorful language used to express the message. The relevance of the Christian church must not be left to perceptions, alone. Perceptions have influencing power, which at times may negatively impact people's lives, and their thinking. There is also a great need for some attitudes changings to occur. I am not talking about the attitudes of those outside folks who are trying to get into the church. No, I am speaking to those church members inside the church that won't let those outside folks into the church. Now you may say, who is it that won't let people into the church? Our doors are always opened! Sure, the doors are opened, but you have some church people so strict in their defense of the church that they don't provide a welcome atmosphere for the ones that don't fit their image of church people. In their minds, they are to guard church dignity, maintain a higher-standard community image, and keep the church sacred for the Lord. They take pride for their efforts in keeping the house of God from street folks.

Before you form the impression that I am criticizing church order, and required decorum, or belittle people for having standards, I am not! Allow me to emphasize this point. The church needs members with love in their hearts for all people. Members, who are more like greeters with smiles, warm personalities, and pleasant to engage. Such people make church, a welcomed place. The sanctity of the church must always be preserved with reverence. It would be out of spiritual order to treat the church like it was a playground. Foolishness should not be tolerated in the church. Saving souls is the mission of the church. It is the business of the church.

Therefore, let the church doors be opened to receive those who drink and/or drunk, the drug pushers and users, the pimps and prostitutes, and all others with addicted vices. Whosoever will let them come! But let them come with the understanding that the church is still God's house. Let them come because the light of God's love is shining on them. Let them come because of the emptiness of their souls need spiritual filling. Let them come seeking salvation. And when they arrive, let them find God's forgiving presence available to transform their lives. Let them see, and know that the church of the living God has opened doors with welcome mats stained with the blood of the lamb.

The church represents hope, life, and spiritual security. Therefore, it must remain an opened door invitation welcoming all who come seeking salvation. This spiritual invitation represents hope, life, and spiritual security. It was given by Jesus. He said, "Whosoever will come after me, let him deny himself, and take up his cross and follow me," (Mark 8:34, KJV). "And the Spirit and the bride say come, and let him that heareth say come, and let him that is athirst come, and whosoever will, let him take the water of life freely," (Revelation 22:17, KJV). Without members having the spiritual attitude to welcome the "whosoever will" into the church, their restrictive attitudes will keep the church stagnant with the faithful few members. It is the kind of attitude that sounds like good church practices, but lacks the attraction for church growth.

The best attitude for church members, regardless of what position they hold in the church, is the spiritual kind that attracts like a magnet, rather than having the negative kind that repels like weak bug-spray. Now, what I have said may be a little exaggeration of some church behaviors. However, attention need to be placed on how we represent the church, our relationship with God, and our spiritual walk with God. There is a desperate need for spiritual examples of what walking with God looks like.

Abraham's relationship with God provides the best biblical example of what it means to walk with God. According to Genesis CHAPTER 12, Abraham, who was named Abram when he came to know God, lived in a city named Ur with his father. The whole family later settled in a place called Haran. It was there that God spoke to him. God told Abram to get his wife and servants and leave Haran and go to a place He would lead him. It was a faith movement. Abram and his wife Sarai had no children. At the time God spoke to Abram, he was 75 years old. Imagine what Abram thought when God invited him to walk with Him with the promise that He was going to make him the father of a great nation. God said, "I will make of thee a great nation, and I will bless thee, and make thy name great; and thou shalt be a blessing," (Genesis 12:2, KJV). Abram began his faith walk with God, going, and not knowing! That's faith.

As Abram journeyed through several countries, some friendly, and others hostile, his relationship, and his walk with God became more defined. Abram had a vision wherein God affirmed His promise of making him a great name. Abram was perplexed because he and his wife Sarai had no children of their own. His first interpretation of the vision was that a servant's child born in his household would represent the promise. God cleared up that misunderstanding. He told Abram that the heir to his legacy would come from his own bowels (Genesis 15). Abram's faith walk was a spiritually transforming process. God changed his name from Abram to Abraham, meaning father of many nations. For God told Abraham that his descendants would become more in numbers than the stars in the sky or the sands on the seashore (Genesis 13:16; Genesis 15:5; Hebrews 11:12, KJV). Abraham became known as the friend of God. This spiritual walk was filled with kindness, generosity, and a genuine love for God. Abraham's walk with God was a growing process. The more time spent with God, the more he learned to trust God. This was evident by his obedience when God told him to take his son Isaac and offer him as a sacrifice. Knowing that such a sacrifice meant killing his son, he trusted God for the life of his son, the heir of promise. His trust and confidence in God proved faith-worthy. Isaac was placed on the altar to be sacrificed. Abraham, positioned with knife in hand, prepared to strike his son's body, when he heard God speak through His Angel telling him "Lay not thine hand upon the lad, neither do thou anything unto him: for now, I know that thou fearest God, seest thou hast not withheld thy son, thine only son from me," (Genesis 22:12, KJV). God provided a substitute which became known as the "Ram in the bush."

God kept His promise to Abraham and gave him a son that was named Isaac. Although Abraham tried to help God fulfill His promise by using Hagar, his wife Sarah's handmaid as a surrogate, God didn't need such help. Abraham and Sarah complicity in this effort brought division into their home, and family. Hagar had a son for Abraham. He was named Ishmael. He was not the child of promise. Yet, through the mercy of God, and kindness shown to Abraham, Ishmael, and his descendants became a great people. They claimed the rights to be identified with Father Abraham.

Isaac grew up and married a woman named Rebekah. They had twin boys who were named Esau and Jacob. Esau was the oldest, and as were their customs, at the appropriate time, the oldest son would receive the greater spiritual blessings. However, Jacob, being younger than his brother, was chosen by God to be heir of God's promise to Abraham. Jacob, known as a trickster, became the victim of tricks played on him by his uncle Laban. Jacob desired, and was promised to have Rachel, the woman of his heart to marry. To his surprise, on the night of his wedding celebration, it was not Rachel given to him, but her older sister Leah. He was tricked by his uncle Laban for two reasons. First, for not knowing their custom for marriage. In their practices, the older daughter must marry before the younger. Second, part of the trickery included the selfishness of his uncle who benefitted from Jacob working for him. God blessed the hand of Jacob. Everything he did prospered. This made Laban both happy, and wealthy. He didn't want to see it end. He promised to give Rachel to Jacob if he agreed to stay with him an additional seven years. Jacob loved Rachel! He stayed.

Following this event, Jacob the trickster became a different man. He became a man that God could, and would use to affirm the promises made to Abraham that his descendants would be more in numbers than stars in the sky, or sands on the seashore. God changed Jacob's name to Israel, the name that would forever identify God's chosen people.

Abraham's walk of faith set the standard from which his descendants developed a spiritual relationship with God. They readily identified with him as the foundation of their lineage, and relationship with God. Abraham's life was proof that Jehovah God, the true and living God, covered them with His presence, and commitment. God promised to bless those who blessed them, and curse those who cursed them. Abraham walked with God. It was a faith-walk. The best example for his descendants to follow.

CHAPTER 7

Elijah Walked with God

T he prophets of old walked with God. They were His spokesmen to the people. It was through their visionary relationship with God, and spiritual leadership, they were able to shape the faith, and understanding of the people of God. There were many notable prophets of the Lord in the Bible, who were known to be great seers. Among such were Prophets Samuel, who crowned David king of Israel. Isaiah, who prophesied more than 800 years before Jesus' birth that He was the coming Messiah. "For unto us a child is born, unto us a son is given, and his name shall be called Wonderful, Counsellor, The mighty God, the everlasting Father, the Prince of Peace," (Isaiah 9:6, KJV).

Jeremiah was called the "Weeping Prophet." He was deeply sorrowed because despite his repeated warnings that Israel's involvement with Egypt would lead to their downfall and captivity, the leaders of Israel refused to believe him. However, as he predicted, Jerusalem was captured by the Babylonians (Jeremiah 32:36, KJV).

Another prophet of distinct notary was Ezekiel. His illustrative message about dried bones in the valley warned the people to return to God. The message was an encouragement for a people whose confidence, and hope in God had been dashed by their conditions, and circumstances. Those dry bones, scattered across the grounds, filled the valley. However, when Ezekiel fervently spoke the word of God, the bones came together, bone to its bone, until they stood up as a mighty army (Ezekiel 37:1-14, KJV). God's concern for His people has always been for the growth of their knowledge, understanding, and spiritual relationship with Him. In spite of their continuous rebellion against God, He never stopped providing them His best accommodations for their living. The illustration of dry bones in the valley were evidence of His commitment to His people. With little spiritual life, and/or devotion to God remaining in His people, He did not give upon them. Instead, He restored them. He continued to call them His own. He made them a mighty nation. The Prophet Ezekiel, in dramatic form, spoke life to a dying people.

Alongside Ezekiel were many other great prophets of God that are not mentioned in this listing. Nevertheless, their services to God were instrumental in keeping the people of Israel reminded that it was Jehovah God who had delivered them out of the hands of the Egyptians. He carried them through the wilderness. He provided them bread, and meat for their hunger, cool water to quench their thirst, and placed them in their land of plenty. The land of promise that flowed with milk and honey. The prophets, these spokesmen, and seers of God were important in helping the people of God grasp, capture, and envision the promises God had for them. Among the many renowned prophets of God, perhaps the one considered the greatest of all, was the man named Elijah. He spiritually walked with God.

Elijah was a colorful prophet that spoke out against the evil practices of his day. He regularly spoke against King Ahab, and his wife Jezebel for their worship of idol gods and their evil influences over the people of God. Elijah was so spiritually attuned in his walk with God that for three, and a half-year, based on Elijah's prayer, God did not let it rain on the earth. When he prayed again, it rained (I Kings 17:1, KJV). Not only that, but his bold faith in God strengthened him to challenge 450 prophets of the idol god Baal to prove to the people who served the true and living God. Baal's prophets were put to shame, defeated, and destroyed by Jehovah, the true and living God (I Kings 18:21-38, KJV). Elijah's walk with God was so true that at his departure, God did not permit him to die. However, two significant things happened. First, because of the spiritual examples he set, his successor, Elisha, received a double portion of Elijah's power from God. Second, Elijah's walk with God allowed him to not see death, but rather he was translated into the presence of God (II Kings 2:11). Elijah was a vivid biblical example of what life looks like when you are walking with God.

In our present time, as it was in the days of old, there lived another great man of God named Elijah. His walk with God influenced many people to change their lives for the glory of God. He became a living spiritual example of walking with God for many people in the state of Alabama, and the city of Tuscaloosa. His spiritual walk with God was both seen, and heard through his preaching, teaching, and religious practice in his relationship with God. This Elijah was none other than the Reverend Dr. Elijah "EJ" James, Jr., Pastor Emeritus of the New Zion Missionary Baptist Church, Northport, Alabama. He served as spiritual leader, and guide of this congregation for more than 40 years. Reverend Gregory Morris now serves as pastor of this spirit-filled body of worshipers. Dr. EJ James was a serving servant of the Lord Jesus Christ. His ministry, and message were about love.

Dr. James loved God. He loved people. He loved touching lives, and making a spiritual difference. As a child, he grew up in the church. He was the son of a pastor. He knew the importance of having a relationship with God. Throughout the many years of his ministry, he made serving people, and the church his spiritual work. It was not uncommon to find him visiting the sick at the hospital, or in their homes. That form of ministry is not so unusual for pastors to do. However, unlike other pastors, Dr. James didn't limit his visitations to his church members only. He made himself available to the community. His personal image was not styled by flashy clothing or dress. He didn't style through the community sporting expensive cars. He always displayed an attitude of humility. Dr. James, like Jesus in His day, did not stand out from the common man. Although, both he and Jesus were characterized by their extraordinary traits. This pastor was always personable, loving, kind, and willing to serve. He served God by serving the people with genuine love, care, and concerns for them. He walked with God.

A noted spiritual change occurred in his ministry work one year after he became ill. It enlightened his spiritual understanding, and expanded his ministry ability. During this incapacitated time, God spoke to him as he prayed, and meditated. He received revelation knowledge about gifts of the Spirit. His spiritual ministry was enriched when God added to his work the gift of healing. It was an epiphany in his walk with God.

From that time forward he continued to preach salvation to the lost, feed those that were hungry, and heal the sick. There was no playing around for him in this spiritual relationship with God. The impact of this spiritual healing ministry caused people to come from near and far to receive the blessings of the Lord. Dr. James' healing ministry was not a "circus" act as some religious people use to exploit people searching for spiritual answers to their pains, hurts, and diseases. He never claimed any power within himself. He believed, and taught that the power of healing was the results of their faith in God.

It was the same kind of faith response that Peter gave the man begging at the temple gate as he and John went to pray. The beggar that sat at the temple gate asking for money received that day a gift of which money could not buy. The gift of being healed. After the man stood up on his renewed legs, he went into the temple walking, leaping, and praising God (Acts 3:6-8, KJV). When the people recognized the miracle that was done, they started worshipping Peter and John, giving them credit for what was done. Peter would have none of it. He quickly corrected the people's adoration. "Why marvel ye at this? Or why look ye so earnestly on us, as though by our own power or holiness we had made this man to walk? The God of Abraham, and of Isaac, and of Jacob, the God of our fathers, hath glorified his Son Jesus …," (Acts 3:11b-13a, KJV).

Dr. James used prayer as the spiritual ministry instrument in healings, casting out devils, and restoring peoples' faith in

God. Not everyone understood his ministry, but that didn't matter. What mattered to him was doing that which God called him to do. He earned great respect from both religious, and civic leaders. He cared about people. He was often seen in the community providing some kind of service, or support to people. It was not beneath him to give strangers a ride in his car, take an elderly member of his congregation to the grocery store, serve as character references, in the courtroom, for a neighbor, friend, or church member. He was a man of God who lived among the people as a servant of God.

He was a great encourager to young people, inspiring them to set goals, and reaching those goals. He believed in education. He earned his bachelor's degree from Stillman College, Tuscaloosa, Alabama as an adult, while being married with children, and working a full-time job. He worked, went to school, and studied at night. He was determined not to allow time, nor circumstances to impede his ability to get a college degree. He earned top honors in his class. His encouragement was always at the heart of helping young preachers, and pastors develop their spiritual skills and gifts. His pastoral doors were always opened to all seeking a closer walk with God.

In the year 2019, at the age of 91, the Lord called His servant home. His life, and legacy are spiritual imprints of why following God makes life in Christ a worthy monument of love. When Rev. Dr. Elijah James died, he was greatly mourned by the Christian community. His death saddened all church folks near, and far who were touched by his love. There was spiritual sorrow for the loss of this great man of God. However, there were also a comforting solace in the hearts of believers concerning this man of God. First, for having known, and shared his life. Second, blessed to have witnessed a true spiritual servant walking with God. Last, but certainly not least, his life, and his love for people served as an example for Christians, and others to follow. His life taught us that walking with God makes all the differences for worship, and for having the love, peace, happiness, and justice that come from knowing God.

Why Walking with God Is Necessary for Love

PART III

CHAPTER 8

Love Will Keep Us Together

L ove remains the most sought-after affirmation of human worth, appreciation, and personal relationships used to verify the meaning of belonging. Regardless of what connections or relationships, the motivation remains the same, finding, or having a love that can be trusted. The way we have learned about love, whether to trust love, or not, is based on ways love has been paraded before us from childhood to adulthood. If love was introduced to us through abusive, or battered relationships, the conclusion will probably yield a reserved acceptance of love. If the love we've seen was cloaked in secrecy with each person involved ducking, and dodging the other as they shared time with others outside of their relationship, trusting love will remain a big question mark. If when you have opened your heart to love, and your lovers, time after time, have left you hurting, and empty, you probably will hesitate to invest your heart in any new love relationships.

Such negatives could leave you questioning whether love is worth the effort, or commitment to trust, or fall in love with anyone ever, or again. Although the pause, or concern for trusting your heart in a love relationship may give you reasons to doubt, or give up on love, don't! You see, the bottom line is this, we need love. We need to give love. We need to receive love. We need to be loved. Without love, emptiness fills the moments, hours, and days of our lives. Love must be the bonding element of the heart. Love will keep families together, and make their homes endearing places to live. Passionate love is required in the hearts of all seeking enduring love relationships. Too often passionate love is reduced to the thrills, and emotions of physical attractions. Instead of the partnership sharing life-long embraces of love, they settle for momentary bliss of ecstasy that neither hold them tight, nor will keep them together, for long. However, there is a love that can be trusted. It is Agape, the God-kind of love that brings true passion to the hearts of all relationships. Through the God-kind of love, spiritual relationships are strengthened, love relationships between men and women are more committed, and strangers receive warm embraces from Christians who walk with the Lord. It is important for Christians' lifestyles to be seen demonstrating God's love in their spiritual walk.

What love can be trusted? This question often robs loving relationships of the comfort and security couples should have in their embraces of each other. Also, children living in homes where love is rarely shared, or expressed are often hesitant to believe in the merits of love. Without an occasional loving embrace, or a tender endearing touch from caring parents, children living such inexpressive relationships, could become mentally scarred, and learn not to trust authoritative love. This concept, or mindset, has also impeded some people from loving God. The love relationship between men and women is often challenged by the word trust! When the phrase, "I love you", is spoken, it evokes such questions as, does this expression comes with genuine respect and commitment? Are those words used as a false entrance into the heart for lust and/ or sexual pleasure? Many people are hurt in love relationships because they dare to believe that love spoken from the lips of their partners is a love that will keep them together in loving embraces.

Unfaithfulness is the temptation to test the waters of interest by outside attractions. Such wavering affections have destroyed many promising love relationships. Trust is a sacred bond. When it is broken, it destroys so much in the love relationship. How do you recover from such a breach? How do you avoid falling into that emptiness? Perhaps the words of the song "Love will keep us together" by the husband and wife singing duo, Captain and Tennille, provides a consoling reminder to all who may think about looking outside of their relationships for love, passion, and sensual pleasures: "You belong to me now. Ain't gonna set you free now. When those girls start hanging around talking me down, hear with your heart and you won't hear a sound; just stop, 'cause I really love you, stop. I'll be thinking of you. Look in my heart and let love keep us together."

Walking with God is necessary in continuous love relationships. Without this spiritual relationship in your love, the glamour, and sweet promises, will soon lose its appeal, and the search for a way out of the relationship will become the daily agenda. Nothing will be right anymore. Spending time together will become meaningless. Lack of conversations between the two of you won't bother you at all. You will feel, and conclude that your romance has gone bad. What's love got to do with it? Perhaps contemporary singer and recording artist Carole King's 1971, top of the chart song, "It's Too Late," provides a sad refrain that best express the responses of couples trying to love one another in a relationship without God. Many tragically comes to this conclusion, "Stayed in bed all mornin' just to pass the time. There is somethin' wrong here, there can be no denyin'. One of us is changin', or maybe we've just stopped tryin'. And it's too late baby now, it's too late, though we really did try to make it. Something inside has died, and I can't hide, and I just can't fake it."

CHAPTER 9

"Husbands and Wives"

Walking with God is necessary for love. There are many references to, and about the subject, and topic of love that speak to human interactions, and personal relationships. Although the word love is commonly used to express feelings, or endearing sentiments, there is not one definition that fits all expressions. Love has many branches of endearments which include, Agape (the God-kind of love), Phileo (brotherly love), Storge (family love), and Eros (erotic, or sexual love). Agape love is unconditional love. That's what God has for us. Phileo love is concerned with caring for, and treating others the way you want to be treated. Storge love is about family bonds, and connections that refuse to be broken by incidents, situations, or circumstances. Eros love is sensual expressions of feelings, wants, and desires. Sexual relationships, and sexual fulfillments are emphasized feelings. Among the different expressions of love, eros gets the most attention in our world today. It seems as though the world is addicted to, and immorally immersed into sexual activities, and sexual expressions. It has been said, "If it feels good, do it." That is one reason many relationships are built around sexual pleasures. This conscious attraction to lewdness makes the biblical standards for sexual engagements outdated. However, God's design for lasting relationships involves sexual involvement that must be engaged in timely embraces, and practiced in the security of love. "Marriage is honourable in all, and the bed undefiled, (Hebrews 13:4a, KJV).

It is said that children live what they learn. If this is true, many of our children living in negative environments are exposed to adult materials, lifestyles, and activities. The introduction of sexual contents into children's lives, way too early, will adversely shape their understanding of sex. This social sex-crazed culture where sex is the major emphasized focus for financial benefits often contribute to the decline of morality, and social mores. There is an urgent need to have strong moral filters, in place, that will ward off the illicit contamination of our children's innocence. These filters include parents monitoring their children's attractions to inappropriate sites, restricting their exposure to adult materials, and be a voice for children's concerns. Parents are to keep children safe from explicit sexual information, and sexual enticements glamorized by revealing fashions, cultural styles.

Unfortunately, people walking in the world's system of information sharing have convinced themselves that prematurely injecting sexual concepts, and sexual awareness to elementary aged children is good education. The significant problem with this way of thinking is that it introduces mature subject-matters to immature children, robbing them of their "innocence." These are our children, our budding gifts, our hope for a better tomorrow. They need to be safeguarded from such sexual information that predators use for immoral indoctrination.

Informed parents, communities, and society must be aware of the extending dangers sex exploitations have on children; their lives, their future. The appealing stimulations of sexual experimentation preyed on teenagers are designed to encourage, and validate their involvement in premarital sexual activities, and sexual acts. There are contrastingly differences between these present social moral views of sexuality, its impact on young people, than past societal moral thinking, and practices which were more restrictive on sexual topics. In this current social sexual culture, children are daily exposed to sensual adult materials, languages, and activities. Previous generations' efforts shielded, and safeguarded their children from provocative, and sexually intriguing information.

In past generations, sexual purity, and being sexually moral were considered to be positive. Being virtuous, and morally fit were admirable, and highly respected character traits. Remaining a virgin until marriage was a valued expected norm. However, times have changed. What once was looked at one way, moral or immoral, has for the most parts been reversed. The sexual challenges facing young people today include not being recognized as a virgin, which differ from the past where being a virgin was a virtue. Being identified as a virgin in the current teenage sexual culture is considered by these young people to be a negative stigma. If a teenage girl, or boy claims virginity as their moral standard, he/she is more likely to be ridiculed than praised by his/her peers.

A contrary approach from world-view positions pertaining to dissemination of sexual information, and sexual relationships is spiritual based principles. The spiritual principles for sexual participation, and sexual purity are Bible-based. These principles are moral, and straightforward. They make sex and marriage bonded partners. Both age, and maturity are emphasized principles for sexual involvements. Then you may morally engage this love expressing activity until your longings are satisfied. However, for people of all ages, that are considering becoming sexually active without meeting the biblical criteria, don't do it! Although being exposed to much illicit sexual materials cause you to become "hot and bothered", and the temptations are there for you to jump into the bed of mischief, again I implore you, don't do it! Instead, be patient with yourself, your growth, and with your development. Soon you will be able to ingratiate yourself, at the right time, and the right principles. Patience will provide you the greatest opportunities to make the right intimate choices. Patience is being willing to wait. Patience will make you mature enough to be successful in life to build your dreams. Patience will make intimacy a worth-while benefit. Therefore, remember this, the spiritual word is, Wait! "But they that wait upon the Lord shall renew their strength; they shall mount up on wings as eagles; they shall run, and not be weary; and they shall walk, and not faint," (Isaiah 40:31, KJV).

The Apostle Paul addressed this understanding in his letter to the churches in Ephesus. In CHAPTER five, his words spoke to the men and women who would become husbands and wives. He emphasized to them that in their tenured love, longevity of their union would become a reality if each person in the relationship submitted one to the other. This submission would guide them through unity of purpose, genuine love, and respect for each other. It is about spiritual honor. Lasting relationships are established on respect. Respect for each other.

Respect for family. Respect for God. When respect is absent, there is no honor in the relationship. Respect strengthens all relationships, and should be valued as necessary in all human interactions.

Couples are more inclined to stay together in loving relationships when each person care enough for what they share, and are willing to make it work. Each person has a submissive role in the relationship. Paul begins by telling wives to submit themselves to their own husbands, as unto the Lord (Ephesians 5:22, KJV). Wives submitting to their husbands sounds like a step back in time when women were treated more like property than partners. Do you remember the wedding vows that many marriages in the past stated? It included the words of commitment for the wife to love, honor, and obey! The word obey has made the word submit appears to be the same in meaning, purpose, and living. One difference between the two words is that obey suggests being a servant, whereas, submit is more of a willing agreement between partners. Submit is a yielding process which allows another person to go ahead of you, go past you, or take a different position. Now before you wives, and women think that I am of the mindset, and/or belief that women are less than men, I say to you, "Hush your face!" None of the kind! Neither does the Apostle Paul. When you follow his instructions, you will know that he is not telling wives to be submissive to their husbands because they are men. Rather, their submissions are to the Lord. It is God who sanctions marriages (Ephesians 5:22b, KJV).

Husbands, in this loving relationship, and in their walk with God, must know that their wives' submission to them is based on their spiritual responsibility toward them. Paul told husbands to love their wives even as Christ loved the church, and gave Himself for it (Ephesians 5:25, KJV). Now, the way Christ loved the church provide husbands the example of how they are to love their wives. Or, why else wives should submit to their husbands? There are three significant elements to the God-kind of love that when applied in marriage relationships, they will keep couples together.

First element. Jesus loved the church unconditionally. This element reveals the kind of love that will not only last, but it will not change in quality, content, or time. It means that there is nothing that we can do, or not do, that will cause Jesus to stop loving us. In like manner, when a husband takes a wife, he is spiritually expected to love her unconditionally. Her faults, her shortcomings, and her inabilities are never reasons or causes for a change in heart. The second element. Jesus loved the church sacrificially. Jesus gave His life on the cross of Calvary as a sacrificial offering for the sins of the world. As the sacrificial lamb of God, His purpose was to restore the broken spiritual relationship between God, and mankind. Jesus paid that price. Disobedience was the sin that severed the spiritual relationship. Restoration occurred when Jesus dying on the cross at Calvary, acknowledged to His Father in Heaven, "It is finished," (John 19:30, KJV). Husbands likewise must demonstrate their love, and commitment to their wives through willing sacrifice. Simply stated, husbands are to put the needs of their wives before their own needs, or desires. The third element. Jesus loved the church eternally. The love of God through Jesus Christ is eternal. God's love is forever. Regardless! So, likewise, husbands should love their wives. Paul stated, "So ought men to love their wives as their own bodies. He that loveth his wife loveth himself," (Ephesians 5:28, KJV).

When husbands love their wives as Christ loves the church: unconditionally, sacrificially, and eternally, then wives can, and often are willing to submit themselves in partnership with the husbands they love. It is through this process that husbands, and wives come together, "For this cause shall a man leave his father and mother and shall be joined unto his wife, and they two shall be one flesh," (Ephesians 5:31, KJV).

CHAPTER 10

Mr. Lonnie and Mrs. Clara Neely

Marriage longevity is no guarantee of a lasting love relationship. It simply means that those couples just didn't leave one another. However, it is refreshing to learn or discover that it was love that kept couples from leaving, divorcing, or just walking away. It was love that kept them together. I found one such couple here in our own town of Tuscaloosa, Alabama. Their names are Mr. Lonnie and Mrs. Clara Neely. As of June, 2021 Mr. Neely reached the age of 103 years old, and Mrs. Neely in September, 2021 became 102 years of age. Their love relationship began when they were young. Their marriage was consummated in 1937. In December 2021 the couple celebrated 84 years of love and happiness. What prompted this long-lasting love relationship? The answer is simple for them. It began with the love, and respect they had for each other. Their walk of faith with God sealed their affection, and care for each other. When asked, what kept them together through the years? Ms. Clara said that "It was the good Lord, and we loved each other." Although having no children of their own, they made themselves available to help other folks raise their children. According to Ms. Clara, there was never a time in their married life that they wanted to get out of their courtship, or marriage relationship. She said, "We loved each other, and we worked together."

This couple's 84 years of marital bliss began in 1937 in a small community where they both lived. They fell in love with each other. As their lives walked through decades, and into a new century, love kept them together. They didn't allow the process of getting older, or birthday numbers restrict their movements, activities, or participations in things they enjoyed doing. They never spent much time traveling to various places or cities, except around local areas supporting their church events. Through the years, their church participation has been a steady involvement, and commitment.

Mr. Lonnie, in his elderly stage of life, still served the church as a deacon. He also remained a faithful singer in the male chorus, and senior choir. He was very active in all facets of the church mission and ministry. He was a cheerful, and kind-spirited gentlemen. He was beloved, and respected by his fellow church members, as well as people throughout the community. Ms. Clara, like her husband sang in the senior choir. Additionally, she worked in the mission ministry department, the Sunday school department, and every other ministry works of the church that needed help in getting the job or project completed. This loving, and most efficient spiritual couple have been faithful members of the Trinity Missionary Baptist Church, Tuscaloosa, Alabama where the Reverend Jessie J. White, Jr. is the pastor.

The Neely's endearing relationship was an inspirational example of love for their church members to observe, marvel in, and imitate. According to Mrs. Marion Bryant, one of the church's most devoted, and actively involved members, "Their expressions of love for each other is a demonstration of an overwhelming tender loving care that they have for one another." Mrs. Bryant observed this dear couple's loving interactions with each other, and how such tenderness influenced a great number of peoples' lives. Her observation of them was that the spiritual impact their love, and genuine care for each other had was a loving positive example that was appreciated by both their church, and the community. Mrs. Bryant, like the Neely's has dedicated much of her life making a difference in children's lives. She, through her biblical teachings, and training of children, applied their examples, and principles of love in her Christian works. Mrs. Bryant, along with the Neely's are known for their unselfish devotion to giving themselves in demonstration of love, and respect for others.

One of many observations she recalled about the Neely's interplay with each other, included a time when they, and other church members, went to eat at a local restaurant. She noted their loving familiarity with each other's food preferences. They would intermittently order food for the other one, in case the one making the selection forgot to include a certain food item. They wanted to make sure that each one got the food items they really wanted. Mrs. Bryant found this loving scene refreshing. Their interactions with each other were like youthful play, young love, tender love, genuine love for each other. This was a reflection of what people should look like when they are in love. The Neely's' long-term love relationship has become a great example for couples investing in love relationships that will last. Mrs. Bryant noted that the Neely's celebrated each other special achievements or awards received. It was joy to them when either one received any kind of praise, gifts, or thanks.

Longevity in marriage does not necessarily mean that the couple stayed together out of love. Perhaps it was their social standing, or position that forced them to remain in a marriage, or relationship that no longer had fire, or fervor. Maybe it was for the sake of children that they didn't want to interrupt their lives by having to explain why their parents were no longer together. Could it had been a fear of being alone, and not finding a sufficient replacement lover? Still could it have been a struggle over financial matters such as having enough to live on? How much pay will come out of the income? How much will be left to live on?

It is good to know that contrary to all those false reasonings for staying together there are a vast number of relationships that came together for love. They are still together because of love. They are willing to stay together in love. For these love relationships, each morning's greetings become an invitation to an evening of great expectations, and love delights. That is why love will keep couples like these together.

CHAPTER 11

Falling in Love with God

Falling in love is an affectionate phrase with the implications of something special, and long-lasting in the hearts of lovers. Falling in love is not a spontaneous emotion that thrills you for a few moments. Rather, it is the process of growing closer in relationships that secure your emotions, and hearts in promised commitments. Likewise, falling in love with God is getting to know Him in spirit, mind, and heart. Falling in love with God brings spiritual meaning, and purpose to a new-born life. This intimate spiritual relationship restores connection with God that was severed when mankind sinned. From that time forward, all humans were born with a sin nature that prevented fellowship with God. Any person can believe that God exists, but without the new birth, which counters the sin nature, there can be no personal spiritual relationship with God.

The new birth in Christ Jesus allows us to love God, to feel God's love, and to fall in love with God. Falling in love with God occurs as you get to know Him. As you learn of His person, nature, and character traits, loving Him will be the natural response. Throughout the Bible there are numerous people whose lives were transformed when, and after, they came to know Him. Such people include the following faith-walkers. Abraham, who in his relationship with God, became known as the friend of God, (James 2:23, KJV). Jacob, after wrestling with the angels all night, had his name changed to Israel. He became known as the father of the Twelve Tribes of Israel (Genesis 32:24, KJV). Moses was restored to a spiritual leadership position, after becoming a fugitive for killing an Egyptian soldier. He was given a new assignment by God to deliver Israel out of Egypt (Exodus 7:2, KJV). Ruth fell in love with God through the shared faith relationship with her mother-in-law Naomi. She later became the great grandmother of David, king of Israel (Ruth 1:16-17, KJV). David loved God for the mercy shown to him, after he had Uriah, a loyal soldier in his army, killed, and took Bathsheba, Uriah's wife, for himself. When his deed was revealed, he asked God for forgiveness, and the restoration of his spiritual relationship with God, "Create in me a clean heart O God; and renew a right spirit within me," (Psalm 51:10, KJV). Along with these mentioned, who loved God, are a vast array of believers with their own stories of tragedies, triumphs, and love. However, the story of an unnamed woman in the seventh CHAPTER of Luke's gospel probably best captures the sentiment of what it means to fall in love with God.

Jesus, and His disciples were the invited guests of a Pharisee leader. His motivation was not to honor Jesus, nor to fall in love with Him. He, like many other Pharisee leaders of his time, was constantly trying to find ways to discredit Jesus, His message, and His movement. Unbeknownst to him, on this day, it would be he, and not Jesus who would be exposed. While they sat eating their meals, this unidentified woman, without an invitation of her own, quietly entered the house of this noted Pharisee carrying an alabaster box of precious perfume. Without words, or an explanation for her being there, she found the place where Jesus sat, and stood behind Him. She poured the precious ointment on His head. She then moved in front of Him, bowed down in submission with tears in her eyes. Tears of joy? Perhaps. Submission? Certain. Repentance? Believed. We know not which. What we do know is that she used those tears to wash His feet, and dried them with her hair. Her love for God was demonstrated by her motivation, her attitude, and her actions toward Jesus (Luke 7:36-38, KJV).

However, her deeds were not without consternation, and resentment by the Pharisee host. His criticism was as mush toward Jesus as it was to the woman. As they sat silently observing the woman's actions, he said to himself, that if Jesus was really a prophet, he would have known that this woman was a sinner. His implications were that Jesus should have known the kind of person she was, and not have had any association with her. Jesus, however, in His loving brilliance, recognized the issue, and wouldn't let this teaching moment pass. He used a parable citing the differences between two people owing a debt. He told the Pharisee host the story about a man's extended goodness toward two people that owed him debts they could not pay. One person owed him five hundred pence, and the other person owed him fifty pence. When they could not pay their debt, he forgave them both. Jesus, then asked the host, "Which one will love him most?" (Luke 41-42, KJV). The Pharisee's response was smug, arrogant, and somewhat dismissive, "I suppose that he to whom he forgave most," (Luke 7:43, KJV).

To the surprise of the Pharisee, Jesus pointed out the differences between his attitude, and the woman's attitude. The differences between his lack of courtesy by not offering Him any courteous greetings, or water to wash His feet when He and His disciples entered the house, and the woman who showed humility, and devotion to Him. By comparison, this Pharisee would have considered himself better than this woman, knowing her past history, and her blemished reputation. However, this woman, whose life was tattered by her lifestyle, and condemned social behaviors, honored Jesus more than the self-righteous host out to defame Jesus. She showed her appreciation for Jesus, who touched her life, and gave her a greater identity. Although her name was not mentioned, she is renowned for having washed His feet with her tears, dried them with her hair, and kissed them. Even though she was known as a sinner, her actions demonstrated that changes had occurred in her life. She was a new creation in Christ. Her many sins were forgiven (Luke 7:44-48, KJV). It was her love for God that motivated her actions, changed her behaviors, and allowed her to receive pardons for her sins. Love will keep us together.

CHAPTER 12

If You Don't Know Me by Now

G oing to church is a common practice for Christians. Worship and praising God each week is a religious ritual for some. For others, it is a time for praising God, and developing a greater spiritual relationship with Him. Walking with God is the process of getting to know God. Understanding God is the avenue by which His calling to spiritual renewal for each of His children is defined. This is evidenced by those who give time to God for prayer, fasting, meditations, and quiet times. They have a greater awareness of God. On the other side, those only being acquainted with God through Sunday mornings worship often only know how to have good church services. Spiritual comparison of the two groups of worshippers finds that the first group's involvement with God will develop within them a trust that will keep them during difficult times, challenging times, dark days-time, and tribulations time. The other group's assessments will often bring doubts as to whether God cares about them. With lack of certainty with God, they will look to other people for solutions.

How is that some people can spend their whole lives going to church, and still not know God? The answer is practical. To know someone, more than by name, or facial recognition, requires spending time with him/her. Knowing someone is not a quick "howdy-do" process. The method of introduction is an external exercise toward meeting someone, and not necessarily beginning a relationship with that person(s). During the introduction phase, you may be enamored, or impressed by the person's appearance, personality, the way he/she presents, and carry him/her self, or simply finding pleasure in the association. That's not really knowing the person.

Relationships established on externals features usually have a short shelf-life. Relationships based on physical attractions will often find limited growth in love relationships, and/or marriages. In like manner, church members having holy appearances, and good records for church attendance, do not confirm that they have personal relationships with God. Church membership, and attendance merely provide them the message, and information to learn the nature of God, the goodness of God, and the love of God. Knowing God takes time. The process of teaching Christians about God, by most churches, include participation in Sunday schools, Bible study, and mission departments groups. Still, without developed spiritual knowledge, and a developed intimacy relationship with God, all participation in church activities become nothing more than religious gymnastics. It is what the Apostle Paul's message to Israel, "For I bear them record that they have a zeal of God, but not according to knowledge," (Romans 10:2, KJV). Knowing God is the spiritual process of receiving knowledge of God that converts the heart, renews the mind, and lives in the soul of those walking with God.

In 1972 four men from Philadelphia, Pennsylvania, musically known as Harold Melvin, and the Blue Notes, recorded a rhythm, and blues song entitled, "If you don't know me by now." This love song spoke of an interaction between a man, and his woman. In the song, she questioned his movements, activities, and faithfulness to her. The man seemed void of understanding as to why she didn't trust him, even when he came home late at night. He challenged her questioning with words that sounded more like the end, rather than a lasting relationship. "If you don't know me by now, you will never, never know me." He goes on to tell her that out of all the things they've been through she should have understood him, like he understood her. After a twenty-year relationship, he told her that she needed to get herself together, or they might as well say good-bye, because "If you don't know me by now, you will never, never, never know me!"

The heart of this song is about trust. Can you trust someone you don't really know? This same question can be directed to church members. All church people do not know God. Therefore, their relationship with God is limited, or not at all. Can you trust God if you don't know Him? In effective spiritual relationships, Christians know how to talk to God. They know how to relate to God. They know how to trust Him. For those not sharing this spiritual relationship, they often have difficulties trusting God; even though they attend church regularly.

The melody, and sweet rhythm of the Harold Melvin, and the Blue Notes' song, coax listeners into hearing the voice of the man, in the song, who instead of sounding like a man in love, appears to be a reprimand of his woman. Assumptions brought them to this conflict in the relationship. Did she not know his heart? Had their relationship been about what was thought rather than what was known? His plea to his love was based on all that they've been through. His disappointing echo was simply this, "If you don't know me by now, you will never, never, ever know me." Well! What about assumptions? Did he assume too much in thinking that his activities, and late hours schedule should not be questioned? Did he assume too much that unspoken love would be interpreted as still faithful, trustworthy, and love? Perhaps the statement of trust made by the man in the song should be reversed to him by his woman. "If you don't know me by now ..." Among the many issues the song suggests this couple had, perhaps the most important one is that of communication, or lack thereof. Poor communication will erode the joys, happiness, and security of many love relationships.

As in the song previously discussed, a few too many church folks have made assumptions about God because they don't know Him. Some may have assumed that God just want them to join church, or go to church. Even after all these years, and from all the study groups attended, sermons heard, God's loving purpose for their lives is not grasped, or understood. Perhaps, they've assumed that God is only needed for hard times. All other times belong to them for their leisure, pleasure, and what feels good. The sad refrain of the Blue Notes' song lingers in the air over the shallow understanding of God. "If you don't know me by now ..." How is it that some people can sit in church Sunday after Sunday hearing about Jesus, and not become motivated to personally know Him? Jesus was a healer, deliverer, teacher, friend, and most importantly, a savior. Hearing His story time after time should stir up spiritual interest.

Jesus' parable about Lazarus, and the rich man spoke of the conversation between the rich man, that died, and Father Abraham, who is representing God. The rich man, having been tossed into hell because he failed to believe in God, is heard begging for mercy. His plea was too late. None was available for him. At the time of his death, he had dismissed the need-to-know God. After death, it was too late for confessions, and acceptance for his benefit. However, he requested, for his brothers who were yet alive, that they be warned to know God. "Abraham saith unto him, They have Moses and the prophets; let them hear them. And he said, Nay, father Abraham: but if one went unto them from the dead, they will repent. And he said unto him, if they hear not Moses and the prophets, neither will they be persuaded, though one rose from the dead," (Luke 16:29-31, KJV). The Bible provides spiritual revelation, and spiritual information about the character of God: His love for the world (John 3:16), His commitment to His people (Hebrew 13:5b), His position of reverence (Exodus 20:3), and His desire for us to learn of him, and to know Him (Matthew 11:29-30).

As a follower of God through Jesus Christ, my encouragement is for all to know Him! His arms are opened to all that seek Him. Salvation is the free gift of God to all who will receive it. If you desire this gift which will transform your life, you must be willing to seek His face, turn from your wicked ways, hear from heaven, be forgiven for sin, receive spiritual healing that will liberate yourself, as well as the land that you love (II Chronicles 7:14). Therefore, knowing God requires a commitment to study the Word of God for growth, and to show yourself approved of Him (II Timothy 2:15).

PART IV
WHY WALKING WITH GOD IS NECESSARY FOR PEACE

PART IV

CHAPTER 13

"Peacemakers Amongst Peacebreakers!"

On the night of Jesus' birth Heaven, and Earth rejoiced. The angels shouted to the world this joyous news, "Glory to God in the highest, and on Earth peace, goodwill toward men," (Luke 2:14, KJV). This message of peace of which the angels proclaimed on that night remains the message of hope for peace today in a world consumed with dangers, violence, and hatred. This criminal-laced atmosphere of negative attitudes produces high rates of crime, and civil hostilities that ravish communities vying for peace, and safety. There is a need for countering influences to spiritually provide people courage to stand up against such evils that rob them of their abilities to feel comfortable, and safe on their own streets, and in their homes. What's needed are people of faith, messengers of God, with strong voices to speak peace that will calm troubled minds, and spirits. That which is needed are church folks who walk with God to speak spiritual messages of truth, faith, and hope that challenge the volatile atmosphere of bitterness, and hatred.

The spiritual influences of churches on communities, and in society have declined in recent years. Please note, I am not saying that the power in the church has been lost, or lessen. Rather, I believe that fewer members have committed themselves to the spiritual mission of walking with God. Jesus, during His teachings one day, challenged the crowd that followed Him to commitment. His words sounded so demanding of their services to God that "From that time many of His disciples went back, and walked no more with Him," (John 6:66, KJV). Although there are churches, it seems like on every corner, their impact, or influences on these peacebreakers have not impeded their torment of local communities, and societies. There is nothing wrong with these churches, or lacking in their spiritual message of peace, but every good message needs good, and faithful messengers. On that night of Jesus' birth, it was the angels from heaven.

Today! The church, and Christians everywhere are entrusted to shout the good news of salvation, and peace. This mantle of hope is given to those who have fallen in love with God. Peace on earth is the settling message of love that causes people of diverse races, and socioeconomic status to embrace others. Peace is what the Christian distinction reflects. Jesus said, "Peace, I leave you, my peace I give unto you: not as the world giveth, give I unto you. Let not your heart be troubled, neither let it be afraid," (John 14:27, KJV). This peace of God that passes human understanding is found in the hearts, and minds of those walking with God. When the troubles of this world seem too large to handle, and at times overwhelming, knowing God can provide the peace needed to endure the storms.

The disciples of Jesus were able to witness this example of peaceful calm one night when they were caught in a storm. Jesus was onboard, asleep. Fear, fright, and doubt were among the emotions experienced by them. Whether they would survive this storm was the major question on their minds. One amazement to me about this story is that the people involved were not novices at sea. Several of them were fishermen, and traveling by waters were common transportation during this time in history. Yet they had no peace in this storm. They even wondered whether Jesus cared if they died in this storm. Walking with God builds faith and confidence that whatever storms encountered, God will make a way for you, either out of the storm, or will get you through the storm.

The kind of doubts, and concerns His disciples entertained in this storm is reflective of how some Christians' approach, and deal with the challenges they face. It is easy to boast of having faith to trust God in stormy times when there are no storms. However, when those stormy times come, the question becomes, will your faith keep you standing? Spiritual growth, and development are key ingredients in Christians' walk with God. Wait! Before you start assessing your faith, and strength based on other people's actions or responses during their difficult times, consider your own life changing, and / or life altering situations. This assessment of faith is about you, and no other folks. Therefore, will your faith master your uncertainties? Walking with God in peace, regardless of the storms, requires continuous personal growth, and spiritual development. The Bible warns believers not to become satisfied, or complacent because things are presently going well with them. Challenging storms could be on the horizons. The writer of Proverbs says that a good pattern to follow, or good example to pay attention to are ants. Yes, I said ants! "The ants are a people not strong, yet they prepare their meat in the summer," (Proverbs 30:25, KJV). Before storms rise, walking with God will prepare you for coming challenges.

The peace you need to calm storms in your life comes from your relationship with God through Jesus Christ. In anxious moments when fear enters your mind, remember, as did His disciples on that stormy night, Jesus is onboard! With this recognition and acknowledgement comes victory, contentment, and peace, regardless of the situation, or storm. When Jesus was awakened, and questioned as to whether He cared about the safety of His disciples. Without conversation, He spoke to the winds, and the waves, "Peace be still." They ceased their torturous activities, (Mark 4:37-39, KJV). There was peace! When you walk with God, His voice will always speak to your hurt, "Peace I leave with you, my peace I give unto you: not as the world giveth, give I unto you. Let not your heart be troubled, neither let it be afraid," (John 14:27, KJV).

CHAPTER 14

"Peace for A Troubled Man"

According to the Bible, in the fifth CHAPTER of Mark, there lived in the country of the Gadarenes, a troubled man whose behaviors was considered by most of the towns' people to be that of an insane person; dangerous, and out of control. He often stayed in the cemetery, and was routinely heard making screaming noises, and hollering as though he was in agony and pain. While he received scorn, rejection, and ridicule by those aware of his actions, it is my assumption, that he was not looking to do harm to anyone. Rather, or perhaps he was simply seeking peace. Far too often we misdiagnose people's needs based on what we perceive, by their behaviors, as being unacceptable and out of control. One of the many concerns in life, in dealing with human behaviors, is that most people have little tolerance, patience, or willing desire to deal with people considered to have behavioral problems. As a result of this mindset, many people with behavioral problems, and personal issues are placed in institutional programs, or some medical facilities.

I recently read an article written by Ms. Meirav Devash, a health and wellness expert, who addressed the subject of Major

Depressive Disorder (MDD). According to Ms. Devash, in this article, MDD is described as being a "sneaky" symptom of mental diseases, and it quietly brings attention to the issues of depression which often go unnoticed. It creeps into the person's mind, and gradually affect his mood, as well as harm, or interfere with his quality of life. Some of MDD's symptoms, according to Ms. Devash, include losing interest in things you once enjoyed, having trouble sleeping, experiencing sudden crying spells, withdrawing from others, hopelessness, and thoughts of self-harm, or suicide. The man in the tomb was not diagnosed as to having MDD, but his behaviors certainly suggested some association.

Therefore, the church must be sensitive to varying behaviors people display so as to provide them the attention, guidance, and love needed to help them with their problems. Walking with God does not make you, or me medical experts in any way, nor does it require you, or me to play one on tv, or in the church. What is required of those who walk with God is to remain sensitive to the needs of others. They must provide necessary, and available assistance in areas where medical services are determined. The church of the Lord Jesus Christ has been stationed in life to be a haven of hope, and salvation. The church is to be a clinic of peace for people with troubled minds, and souls. Imagine, if the people of Gadara had gone to the man in the tomb with kind words, and loving spirits, rather than approaching him with fear, perhaps the man's agony wouldn't have been prolonged, and seemed hopeless. Thank God for Jesus who took time to address this man's needs. He needed peace!

It was early in the morning when the ship that carried Jesus, and His disciples crossed over the sea, and landed on the shores of the Gadarenes. Of all the people in the town that noticed their arrival, it was the man in the tomb. When the man in the tomb saw Jesus from afar, he ran toward Him as though he was a bull charging a matador in a bullfight ring demanding an answer as to why Jesus had come there. He asked Jesus, "What have I to do with thee, Jesus, thou Son of the most-high God? I adjure thee by God, that thou torment me not," (Mark 5:7, KJV). Torment! Torment! Torment! That's what this man was used to receiving. That's what he's been conditioned to expect from people. No help! No support! No peace! Just torment! Torment! Torment! Jesus recognized the man in the tomb's condition, and spoke not to his behavior, but to his need. He needed relief.

The man in the tomb wrestled with demons. When Jesus commanded the demons to come out of the man, He asked their names. The demons replied, "My name is Legion, for we are many," (Mark 5:9b, KJV). When the man was relieved of the torture he endured, he was found to have peace! After the people of Gadara heard about what happened, they came to see the new man for themselves. When they found him, they noticed that his behaviors had changed. He was sitting and clothed, and in his right mind, (Mark 5:15b, KJV). Instead of the town's people rejoicing over this dramatic change in this wild-man's life, and that he was no longer out of control, they were afraid of him. Unfortunately, too often we find in our social interactions, similar reactions by church people toward those who have lived ungodly lifestyles. Although Jesus may have changed their lives and transformed their identities, the reality of rejection by church folks caused some, feeling rejected, to look for acceptance from people, or groups outside of the church. Rejecting people because they don't fit our requirements for participation must not be regarded, perceived, or thought to be the true Christian, or Godly attitude of the Church. Jesus said that His house shall be known by all nations as the house of prayer, (Matthew 21:13). Therefore, in the House of God, forgiveness, love, and peace must always be found available to all that are seeking safety, refuge, deliverances, and hope.

Walking with God in troubled times provides peacemakers the urgency to speak with calming voices that will quell violent, dangerous, and out of control situations. These spiritual voices speak with the love of God, and give respect to all that will hear, and receive their messages. Voices of peace will always calm the storms. The Apostle Paul's letter to the Philippians' churches reminded them of the strength that they have in God through peace. He encouraged them to not worry over things, but to trust God. No matter how difficult it may seem, the peace of God will sustain them. He told them to "Be careful for nothing, but in everything by prayer and supplication with thanksgiving let your requests be made known unto God. And the peace of God which passeth all understanding shall keep your hearts and minds through Christ Jesus," (Philippians 4:6-7, KJV).

In this world of belonging, and living the hopes, and dreams of your existence, there are opposing forces that will impact the process of reaching your desired levels of prosperity, and success. These forces are labeled, good and evil, and they are directed by people considered to be either, peacemakers are peacebreakers. Note, they are not the same. Neither is their focus the same. They differ in all ways: one builds up, the other tears down. One promotes life, the other damages, or destroys life. One support success, the other foster failures. One can be considered spiritual, and the other known to be worldly. Peacebreakers are opposite of Peacemakers.

Peacebreakers are individuals, and sometimes groups whose mission, agenda, or purpose is to disturb the calm. Peacebreakers seize opportunities to create divisions among church members, family members, citizens, and other groupings of people. Many peacebreakers are like the man in the tomb, wrestling with demons. How else do you explain why so many young people in this generation of youths have such devious hostilities toward law and order? Their violent actions toward one another, which involve using unlawful guns, and illicit drugs leave so many of them dead, and too many of them going to jail. How else do you explain the hate attitudes of people who hide behind racial masks, while pretending to be friends? They are readily shielded by unjust laws, protected by law enforcement, and given implied approval for their actions. These peacebreakers use fear to terrorize minority communities through violence, and intimidations. Such actions suggest that these people are possessed with bitterness! Possessed with hatred! Possessed with fear! Possessed with insecurities! These kinds of possessions would be considered, by the standards of the man in the tomb, as being "demon" possessed!

These peacebreakers are not only outside the church, some are considered to be faithful church members, and regular church attenders. Church members that, at times, are viewed as peacebreakers because of their disagreeable behaviors, and attitudes, often don't see themselves as being either negative, or destructive. Many of them have the opposite view of what they do. Fair, or not they usually believe that their actions are glorious, good, right, and justified. Such was the thinking of prominent religious groups in the time of Jesus. His ministry on the Earth was spiritually challenging to the established religious organizations to the point that they openly opposed His ministry works.

According to the Bible, the Jewish religious orders, of which the Pharisees and Sadducees were the primary religious authority, thought they were right in putting down the teachings, and works of Jesus' ministry. From their positions, they did not see themselves as working against God. They convinced themselves that they were the agents of God. It was their duty to keep the temple of God sanctified by opposing false teachers, and their teachings. It was their duty to prevent false religions from diverting the attention of God's people, and the pollution of their spiritual interests. This protective form of religious practices produced Saul of Tarsus. He was a law-keeper, and would not tolerate any lawbreakers. Although the laws given by Moses were good, the keeping of them were difficult. Also, the law could not give life, only punishments.

The Apostle Paul provides clarity to this emphasized point of religious protection. When he was known as Saul of Tarsus, he was a Pharisee, and a member of the Sanhedrin Council, the ruling religious authority in the Jewish religion. He was greatly used by the religious orders to halt the development, and movement of Jesus' followers. They became known as people of "This Way." It was during this assignment, on the road to the city of Damascus, where Saul had orders to arrest anyone that identified him/herself as a follower of Jesus. However, Saul's vengeful journey was interrupted by a spiritual light from Heaven which knocked him to the ground. He heard God speak to him in a voice that questioned his purpose, "Saul,

Saul, why persecutest thou me?" (Acts 9:4b). Saul was unsure as to who it was that was speaking to him. He asked, "Who art thou, Lord?" (Acts 9:5a, KJV). Shouldn't he had known who it was that was speaking to him? If he was so determined, on this crusade, to preserve the dignity, and deity of God from these supposed to be religious outlaws, as they were portrayed. Shouldn't he had known that this was God? Religions can, and often do, blind their followers to spiritual truths.

Fortunately for us, and for the growth, and expansions of the Christian church, Saul was religious, but not hardhearted. He was not resistant to being spiritually changed. His heart was true for God, although his mind was clouded with insufficient knowledge of God. This was evident by the fact when he heard God speak, and knew it was God speaking to him, he repented. He became a true follower of Jesus' teachings, ministry, and mission. His faithful work for God as Paul the apostle was instrumental in teaching gentile believers, alongside the Jews, to walk with God in peace, and with one another.

CHAPTER 15

"Blessed Are the Peacemakers"

P eace is what the world needs. Jesus taught His disciples in the Sermon on the Mount this great truth, "Blessed are the peacemakers, for they shall be called the children of God," (Matthew 5:9, KJV). Peacemakers! People who are committed to the efforts of establishing, and maintaining peace in the home, church, community, and the world. Although peace is what the world needs, and what is hoped for against violence, it remains a difficult task to achieve. Among the reasons for this difficulty toward achieving peace is the contrast between the fear of peacemakers, and the devious works of peacebreakers. Therefore, as long as peacemakers walk by sight, and not by faith, or are guided by their feelings, rather than by their commitment, or have the desire to be people pleasers, rather than stand on spiritual principles, peacebreakers will continue their violent tirades, and peace will remain an unachieved goal.

We live in a world filled with hostilities, and violence. Although America is renowned to be the home of the brave, and land of the free, violence has been, and remain a dominate concern for many of her citizens' safety, and security. Among the many problems that fuel the unrest, and uncertainties in society are increased acts of violence, systemic racial discriminations, socioeconomic differences, impoverished lower-income communities, and a legal justice system that fails to enforce unbiased laws. According to the preamble of the U.S. Constitution, America is "One nation under God, indivisible, with liberty and justice for all." If peace is to be achieved these words must become deliberate practices at all levels of authority without favoritism, or biases.

In spite of America's shortcomings in these areas of great concerns, she remains the best hope in the world for establishing and providing her citizens the opportunity for equality of life. The influences of peacemakers in America's history have helped to shape this hope, and possibility that one day, America will truly become one nation under God. The trails of peace made by these peacemakers are narrow, and their number is not as large as peace movements demand. However, the imprints of their devotion as peacemakers are deeply etched into our hearts. Throughout history, peacemakers have been bold, strong, and committed to the cause of justice, and peace. Names that fit into this category of recognition, are extensive, and need to be mentioned. They need to be thanked. They should be honored, and appreciated for their contributions to peace, and safety. History has recorded them all. Historians have written down many of their names, but not all. That is why I would like to add to the list of peacemakers the name of a man who has proven himself indeed of being a peacemaker. His name is Severn "Sebo" Sanders. He is Deputy Chief of Community Policing in the Tuscaloosa Police Department, Tuscaloosa, Alabama.

CHAPTER 16

"Deputy Chief 'Sebo' Sanders"

Becoming police officers, for some applicants, is but an opportunity to get or have an important civil-service job. However, for Severn "Sebo" Sanders, Deputy Chief of Community Policing in the Tuscaloosa Police Department (TPD), who was inspired by his grandfather's career as a policeman, considered his application for the job to be more of a confirmation from God. His grandfather, Mr. Sam Sanders, the first black police officer in the city of Marion, Alabama, played a significant role in his decision to enter law enforcement. The wisdom of grandfather Sanders, a man of deep faith in God, taught Sebo, as he is affectionately called, to do right, and to always treat people right. Chief Sanders has put into practice this spiritual principle both as a person, and as a police officer. As the chief of community policing, his main focus is on developing positive relations between police and the community. He is aware that as long as people are negatively engaged with police, or have negative perceptions of police intentions, there can be no peace between them. Because of this lack of trust or positive interactions, many, if not most incidents involving police in the community often escalate into violent or negative confrontations. Based on this concern, this community relations proposed program was created, and designed to reduce existing frictions between the police, and communities they serve.

The combination of being both a policeman and a peacemaker may be a difficult task to achieve for some people, but not so much for Sebo who has throughout his career worked hard to eliminate the frictions among people in the community. That is why he being selected as chief, of the recently established community policing department, was the best choice for this community relations operation. According to the Chief, he enjoys being a police officer because he likes being able to make a difference in the lives of people in the community. During his 25 years on the TPD force, Chief Sanders has seen and understands the importance of developing positive levels of trust between police and public so as to reduce crimes and violence in communities.

Chief Sanders' motivation, and care for community safety is to ensure that all people, regardless of race, creed, or color, are able to enjoy the best quality of life without fear of violence, intimidation, or unlawful activities occurring in their communities. He believes that the best way to attain peace, and maintain safety in communities is for all participants: the police, law enforcement persons, and citizens in communities come together, work together, and become peacemakers together. His desired aim has been to make all communities in Tuscaloosa safe, and crime free. He wants Tuscaloosa to be known as, and perceived to be a welcoming place. A city, prospectively, like Mayberry on the Andy Griffith show, where people who come to this town from other places, will feel the security of the city, and positively engage the varied communities.

Chief Sanders, as peacemaker, often finds himself trying to resolve conflicts, and confrontational situations; especially when people don't have knowledge of the law. He works hard to deescalate the volatile settings by first of all encouraging citizens to comply with police officers' directives, and second, not to resist their commands. He makes known to community members that bad policing will not go unchecked, but proper protocol must be practiced. He goes out of his way to educate the community about the law, and what should be their proper responses. Peacemaker Sanders, one day during his work in the community found two neighbors in a heated argument. Rather than dealing with the situation strictly from a law enforcement perspective, he brought the neighbors together. He talked to them, reasoned with them, and reminded them that they have to live together. It was important for them, and the community to resolve the negative issues between them and be good neighbors together.

Chief Sanders is a role model for the young, and old. He believes, as he says, "If I don't get out and lead by example others will not do it." During his 25 years at TPD, the Chief of Community Policing has made himself available to speak to young people. His motivation is to help them redirect their focus, and attitude from negative influences. His intention is to make them aware of, and recognize opportunities they are given to recover from their mistakes. Bethel Community Outreach is one of many programs he routinely attends. This educational outreach program is designed to provide students in grades 6-12, who were suspended, or expelled from the public-school systems, a second chance opportunity. These students' behavioral problems, or violations of schools' zero tolerance policies had caused them the privilege of attending their schools.

Bethel Community Outreach program is housed in Bethel Missionary Baptist Church where Reverend Schmitt Moore is the pastor, and serves as Board Chairman of this educational outreach program. Project B.E.T.H.E.L. is aptly named for its purpose of Bringing Education To Help Expelled Learners. The daily operations of this community outreach program are under the supervision of its executive director, Mr. Tommy Woods, a retired school principal, and Mrs. Maxine D. Abrams, retired classroom teacher, who provides exemplary leadership as director of Project B.E.T.H.E.L. She is administratively accompanied by highly qualified, and skilled retired educators who have served in classrooms, and administration positions. Among these retired educators are Mrs. Octavia Miles, and Mr. Rush Howard. They have both been in the classroom, and held administration responsibilities. The other retired educators, who have dedicated their knowledge, skills, classroom experiences, and educational proficiency to aid these students' rehabilitations are Mrs. Sallie Cook, Mrs. Bessie Harper, and Mrs. Veronica Williams. Mrs. Hassie Bailey provides office support to this outreach program. These highly skilled educators have committed their professional knowledge, and determined efforts to help troubled students meet standards, and requirements to return them back to their respective schools. Additionally, motivational speakers from various professions are routinely invited to encourage students to change, adjust, or modify their behaviors. Chief Sebo Sanders has for 20 years been one of those highly sought, and used professional speakers for this program.

Whenever Chief Sanders speaks to the students at Project BETHEL, he makes his presentations, and interactions with them real life consequences. Students are exposed to the truth about the long-term consequences of poor, or bad decision-making. Chief Sanders believes that it is his responsibility to speak truth about life issues to the students listening to him. He constantly emphasizes to students that the life they are facing is filled with challenges that they need to be prepared to deal with. His presentations to them highlight the dangers they should avoid, including drug use, selling, and association with people who are negative influences for them. He warned them of consequences for handling, possessing, and using unlawful guns, or weapons which often lead to gun violence. He emphasized to them the unnecessary number of young people being killed, or going to jail behind guns improperly used.

He believes that this straightforward, and no-nonsense interaction with students yield the best results. Although not all students capitalize on the second chances, that they are provided through programs such as Bethel Community Outreach, Chief Sanders says, "There are successes to be proud about." Quite often students, and former students of the program have come to him in public places to let him know they remembered him speaking to them. Some shared the success they achieved in school, and in life because of his straightforward, no-nonsense presentations. Chief Sebo Sanders is a peacemaker who makes a difference in a world filled with dangers, fears, hostilities, and violence. The teachings of Jesus best sum up the value and importance of people, men and women, who like Deputy Chief Sanders are committed to providing safety, security, and peace in communities. This partnership requires changes in attitudes, motivation, commitment by both law enforcement persons, and the communities they encounter. Jesus said, "Blessed are the peacemakers for they shall be called the children of God," (Matthew 5:9, KJV)

Chief Sanders is a dedicated police officer, professional civil servant, exemplary leader, role model, concerned citizen, a loving person, and a great individual to know. He is a peacemaker. He is determined to make his department, Community Policing at TPD, an effective operation, and a great success. It may not be perceived as such, right now, but one day, through his drive, motivation, leadership, prayers, and commitment to unity of purpose, this city he patrols, and protects, Tuscaloosa, Alabama, may soon be as revered, peaceful, and crime-free as the city of Mayberry on the Andy Griffith show.

PART V
WHY WALKING WITH GOD IS NECESSARY FOR HAPPINESS

PART V

CHAPTER 17

Happiness

Sorrows, and sadness are feelings. They are displayed gestures that often dominate expressions and emotions of troubled people. Frowns, and scorns are facial pictures that suggest their unrest, discomfort, disagreements, and unhappiness. Happiness is the sought-after desire most people look for in their relationships, including romances, marriages, friendships, and personal acceptance. It is said by some people that happiness is a choice. If this explanation for happiness is true, then why is this much desired element of human interactions so elusive to have, keep, maintain, and share? It is my assessment that happiness is more than simply making a choice to be happy, it is the spiritual need to connect with God. He is the true meaning of happiness. If true happiness, real happiness, unpretending happiness is to be achieved, received, and shared, God must be in it. Happiness is sheltered in love. "God is love," (I John 4:8b, KJV).

Walking with God in spiritual relationship will produce and/or develop joy, and happiness in the lives of people engaged in the process. The relationship will provide a joyous spirit of satisfaction. There are people who permit themselves to become bogged down in works, and activities that are purposed to bring happiness, only to discover that works alone are unfulfilling. Far too many people are misled to engaged in this approach seeking happiness, and end up having little to no joy in their lives. Pretending joy is often illustrated on smiling faces purposely structured to give false impressions of happiness, or of being happy.

Customer service, in public businesses, is almost a lost benefit when it comes to giving customers the quality services they deserve. The loss of these gratuitous services often leaves customers regretting interactions with these none-empathetic employees. Many of them don't seem to enjoy their work, and demonstrate little evidence that they find any happiness in their jobs. Recently I went into one convenient store. As a matter of fact, I was the first one at the door when the clerk unlocked the door. Three employees were upfront. I greeted them with a hearty "Good morning!" The three employees that were lounging around the checkout counter responded with a lackluster reply. Instead of being concerned about what I needed, or whether I knew where to find the product I was seeking, they were collectively complaining about their work schedules. It was clear to me that among them, there was no happiness in working this job. The clerk that checked me out did not offer me a smile, nor a cheerful word of encouragement, such as "Have a good day." It made me feel as though I was just, to them, an unimportant figure that invaded their time of moaning, groaning, and complaining. There definitely was no happiness among this group. Happiness comes from joyful hearts that is within you, and cheerfully expressed through your manners, and mannerisms.

CHAPTER 18

The Work of Martha, and The Heart of Mary

Mary, Martha, and their brother Lazarus were known to be friends with Jesus. During His ministry days, Jesus would often pass through the town of Bethany. While there, He stopped at their house, shared their friendship, and meals. The personalities of Lazarus, Martha, and Mary are diverse in their presentations. Mary appears to be the more outgoing of the two sisters. She did not seem to internalize, or allow things undone to bother her much. Whereas Martha seems to be the detailed member of the family. She liked things to be done in a timely manner, and in an orderly way with everyone pitching in to do their parts. Mary is carefree. Martha is a worrier. Lazarus is presented as the silent type. Even through his miraculous resurrection we do not hear Lazarus' voice. His silence would have left him unnoticed had not his health condition highlighted his story. Before the request came to Jesus from Lazarus's sisters asking Him to come visit, and see about his friend who was very ill, we were introduced to the family at a setting of relaxation.

Jesus, and His disciples were invited to eat at the home of Lazarus, Mary, and Martha. As usual, Martha assumed the responsibility for getting the meal ready. She was busy in the kitchen. It would seem that as much time Martha spent making sure that all the domestic chores were done, that seeing it all come together would be happiness for her. However, as gifted, and skilled she may have been at her chores, there are inklings that she lacked joy, and happiness in doing her tasks. Don't misunderstand me about Martha. I am not saying that she was bitter, or resentful toward what she was doing, but that she lacked the happiness of doing them. She was satisfied in washing, cooking, and cleaning. She was satisfied in serving others. She was satisfied at being a gracious host for friends, and travelers that stopped in for fellowship. She had satisfaction in her life, but not happiness.

As she prepared the meal for her guests, she became frustrated at her sister Mary. There she was a woman working diligently while the men sat together talking, and listening to Jesus. His conversation probably spoke of God's unconditional love for the world. Perhaps the subjects included the importance of having an abundant life, or the necessity of having a personal relationship with God. For Martha, it was okay for the men to sit around in discussion while the food was being prepared. She was accustomed for such settings, but why was Mary sitting there? This frustrated her to the point that she couldn't take it anymore. She had to say something about it. "Lord dost thou not care that my sister hath left me alone to serve? Bid her therefore that she helps me," (Luke 10:40b, KJV). Frustrations will often turn into anger, bitterness, and resentment, if it is not rechanneled to the right focus, understanding, and purpose. Jesus did just that. He knew the value of family. It is important for family members to find strength in one another. It is important for family members not to isolate themselves from each other. Family members must never allow emotions, rebellions, or misunderstandings to bring separations, or divisions between them. Jesus calmed her down in this loving embrace that affirmed her worth to her family, and their friendship. In no way did He demean her, her actions, or her attitude. He gently embraced her. He knew her hurt. He didn't want to add it. His soothing words embraced this challenging moment. Martha! Martha! He called her name. You are worried, and troubled over many things, but you only need one thing (Luke 10:41). These things that you are worrying over, as important as they may be for the moment, will soon be gone. However, what you need to complete your life is true happiness that will last forever. He told her that it was for this reason her sister Mary sat at His feet, listening. "Mary has chosen that good part, which shall not be taken away from her," (Luke 10:42, KJV).

It is not written in the text, but I believe that on this day, her personal relationship, and conversation with Jesus made all the difference. Martha found happiness. It was a spiritual happiness with depth that outweighed emotions, or feelings. It was a spiritual happiness that rested in the joy of worth, appreciation, and respect. Being reconciled in love, this family continued to be a resting place for Jesus throughout His ministry. However, one day, as Jesus was teaching, the sisters, Mary and Martha, sent word for Him to come quickly because their brother Lazarus was gravely ill. Jesus did not leave His work to go right away. Lazarus, the friend of Jesus, being sick, died. End of story, right? No! We know that's not how the story ends!

When Jesus arrived in Bethany, at the home of Mary and Martha. He was greeted by each sister with the affirmed belief that if He had been there Lazarus would not have died. Jesus, feeling the sting of their pain, spoke to them in spiritual renewal language, "I am the resurrection, and the life, he that believeth in me, though he were dead, yet shall he live," (John 11:25a, KJV). Then the miracle occurred. At the grave, He called Lazarus back from the dead, and restored him to his family. There was joy, and happiness.

CHAPTER 19

Madame President

T he cheerful spirit of leaders often gives those following their leadership needed courage, energy, and motivation to efficiently achieve desired goals, or objectives. This personality trait is important for effective leadership. Few leaders utilize it as an opportunity to build stronger, or better relationships with their followers. A cheerful spirit is also a valuable communication tool. Leaders' cheerful spirits become positive encouragement for their followers. It helps them to have positive working attitudes.

Leaders' cheerful spirits do not supersede their responsibility to provide strong, effective, and corrective leadership principles. That is why leaders have to be extremely cautious in how intimately they relate to, and interact with their followers. In this shared relationship, there exists a thin line between friendliness to know them, and sternness that get the work done. If this relationship is not properly balanced, confusion, misunderstanding, rebellion, and even rejection of leadership principles could result. When leaders are mischaracterized as being indifferent, or inconsistent in how they relate to their followers, positive attitudes, self-esteem, and effective productivity are often destroyed.

Therefore, clarity of personal interactions between the two becomes necessary for understanding, and for achieving the agenda. Such clarity will allow subordinates to positively benefit from the working relationship. They will know how to engage their leaders in ways that respect them, rather than having fear of them. Confident leaders will skillfully make known to subordinates how their relationship should be interpreted, or perceived. They will provide clear communication, and understanding to avoid damaging their work relationship, or lose effective productivity. A cheerful spirit comes from personal confidence. Personal confidence produces happiness. Happiness is an indication of having peace within one's self. Leaders that lack this spirit of happiness often pollutes the work atmosphere through their uncertainty, and gloomy personalities. This pollution results in created conflicts, animosity, and unhappiness. A happy leader emits happiness.

Mrs. Maxine D. Abrams is a leader that exude happiness. She knows leadership. She knows how to be an effective leader. She is a leader with a joyous spirit that comes from her relationship with God. She loves people. She knows how to work effectively with people. Throughout her life, she has found herself elevated from one leadership position to another. Whether it has been in her family, community, professional vocation, or church positions. She has always been a leader. Among her present positions of leadership is that of being President of the Alabama State Missionary Baptist Convention's Women's Auxiliary. Her leadership outreach, in this missionary work, covers the whole state of Alabama.

President Abrams' happiness comes from her heart. It is deeply rooted in her faith in God. Each morning she wakes up, and give God thanks for another day. President Abrams is a meticulous leader whose knowledge of skills, and care for people afford her the ability to correct others without causing them to feel debased, or put down. Her joyful personality is magnetic. It draws supporters, and attracts other leaders that are equally excited as she to do the work for God, and the church. These followers work well under her leadership. President Abrams wears a well-earned positive reputation that is highly respected by all who knows her. As president of the women's Auxiliary, her duties, and responsibilities are numerous, challenging, and time consuming. However, through all her activities, she maintains a positive presence in ensuring that all objectives are met at the highest levels of productivity. She is a confident leader who knows how to delegate responsibilities that effectively achieve missionary goals.

President Abrams is a people person. She learned the value of being kind to people, and treating them the way you would want to be treated sitting under the tutelage of her mother, Mrs. Ethel Mae Daniel. This excellent tutor of morals, and dignity, caused President Abrams to proclaim this wonderful woman, the "Greatest Mother" in the world. Mrs. Daniel's kindness, caring spirit, loving heart, and supportive ways that constantly helped others, earned her respect throughout the community where her family lived. This instilled wisdom, and home training given to President Abrams became applied guidance to her life. It made a quality difference towards her ability to work with people. Throughout her professional career, as an educator in the public-school systems, this "skirt-tail" wisdom influenced her to perform her tasks at the highest levels of proficiency; but always with people in mind. Teaching students became her passion. Motivating students to learn through efforts that pursued their academic excellence was her goal, or objective. It meant something to her to bring a smile to a child's face. She knew, and realized that many students faced personal, and home difficulties, at times, that often robbed them of their desired need for happiness.

When it comes to children's happiness, President Abrams has always worked extensively to ensure that sad children are made happy, and happy children are made happier. This practiced acts of love for children did not end when she became a retired educator from the school systems. You see, The Lord still had need for her proficient skills, loving mannerism, and joyful persona. After a short period of exile from the classroom, the longing to engage the lives of young people stirred her heart. It was at this time that Mr. Tommy Woods, Executive Director of a recently established community outreach program designed to help troubled students, reached out to her to become director of this program. Mrs. Abrams picked up this noble mantle of responsibility for several reasons. The most important one being that she was needed for this important work. She was needed to positively impact lives of disturbed students living in, and coming out of troubled homes.

This program was implemented to provide students, that were either suspended, or expelled from schools, a second chance to complete their educational development. She realized that among the many things that students entering this program needed was for their need of someone to care. They need someone to give them reasons to be happy. Students enrolled in this program often come with deep negative attitudes. Their unacceptable behaviors come from the bitterness, hatred, resentments, personal conflicts, and disobedience they had learned. Rebellion is the key protagonist that prevent many of these students from succeeding in the classrooms.

Being rebellious was the justifying platform many students entering this program used to shelter them from the hurt, and pain they felt from some adults, and authority figures that caused them emotional, and psychological injuries. Many students enter the program with their defenses in place. They expect rejections. They knew that possibly they would be labeled with some negative tag. They were prepared to be reprimanded by people in authority. That's what they are often conditioned to believe about the system. That's what they expect to happen. However, contrary to what they may have presupposed or believed would occur when they enrolled into Project BETHEL, what they find, instead, is positive interactions, positive reinforcements, and positive objectives. They are shown love, and respect. They are nourished academically. They are provided positive reasons to change their attitudes, and behaviors.

The changes in these students' perspectives are greatly influenced by this Christian-based outreach program. The posture, or atmosphere for educational learning can be attributed to Director Abrams' extraordinary leadership, and guidelines. She implements, and ensures that all students, while involved in this program would be given the opportunity to succeed. She assures students that they will be treated with kindness, genuine care, concern, and respect. President Abrams' love for these children is matched only by her dedication to ensure them the opportunity to pursue, and achieve their academic goals. She does her best to educationally motivate them to rise up beyond the set-backs that brought them to the program. Her efficient staff of retired educators provide students the educational proficiency they need to aptly meet the academic curriculum requirements.

Additionally, these students are able to study, and be taught in a serene spiritual atmosphere designed to insulate them from frivolous outside distractions. The program focus is on students learning, and returning to their respective schools, and classrooms. Further exposure to educational outlooks, and career opportunities are provided through professionals' speakers addressing them, and sharing their experiences, and qualifications. Students are encouraged to strive for excellence in the classroom, be positive in their attitudes, and not allow poor decision-making to further dictate their personal lives, or behaviors.

President Abrams, the leader of Alabama State women's auxiliary missionary ministry, devotes herself to being a servant-leader. She is not hesitant in involving herself in any, or all designated works, projects, or activities the ministry incurs. She does not present herself, as president, to be too high up in position to do the same works as other women involved in missionary works. According to President Abrams, when certain aspects of work need to be done, and no one is available to do it, she doesn't think it is out of order for her to get in there, and do it herself. Happiness for President Abrams is the delights she enjoys in working with, and having fellowship with missionary women across the state of Alabama. Because her leadership demeanor is built on kindness, and respect for others, the women workers under her leadership supports this concept, and share this attitude. Under her gracious leadership these missionary women take pride in serving, and working arduously to achieve the missionary ministry's projects, activities, and goals. Without coercion, these women of God joyfully carry out their assignments. They do it with her, for her, and to the glory of God.

According to President Abrams, the happiness she finds in the relationships with these missionary women includes the following, shared fellowships they enjoy across the state of Alabama, forming life-long friendships, and enlisting younger women to participate in the missionary ministry. Happiness involves working with missionary women dedicated to setting and attaining spiritual, and financial goals. These missionary women, she engages, are quality servants of God who take seriously their duties, responsibilities, and support. President Abrams prides herself on being a leader that follows leadership. Her responsibility as the women's auxiliary president falls under the leadership, and directives of the President of the Alabama State Missionary Baptist Convention. Walking with God for President Maxine D. Abrams is not a mantra to boast about positions, or achievements. Rather, walking with God becomes testimonies of faith that motivates her life passion. The spirit-filled kind of passion that makes her happy. The God-kind of passion that brings happiness!

WHY WALKING WITH GOD IS NECESSARY FOR JUSTICE

PART VI

CHAPTER 20

... And Justice for All

The American flag is raised each day over national buildings, state houses, schools, and individual homes. This flag represents the pride, dignity, and sacrifices of a nation. It is a sacred reminder, and symbolic recognition of love for a nation, sacrifices for peace and freedom, and the faith of a people who trust in God. As the flag is hoisted in the air, in respect, citizens stand to their feet, soldiers salute, others place their hands to their hearts. This is a moment of reverence. "I pledge allegiance to the flag of the United States of America, and to the Republic for which it stands, one Nation under God, indivisible, with liberty and justice for all." This flag, flying across the nation, and the world, symbolizes that America is still the land of the free, home of the brave. Our constant fight is to ensure that there is freedom, dignity, and justice for all.

Walking with God is a faith walk. It is the pathway of truth, and justice that travels through all roads, and is inserted into all facets of social living. The church, and religious groups have been designated to be expected places where people walking with God are found. God is not restricted to a few organizations. Although walking with God is thought to be reserved for church people, or people in religious organizations, walking with God is a spiritual pathway traveling through every segment of social strata. This even includes the necessity of finding Godly principles, and spiritual tenets in the halls of justice. People who walk with God are needed in courtrooms, and law enforcement offices. It is equally significant for people in other professions to know that walking with God is more than being religious. It is about justice, freedom, and righteous living.

Its principles are applicable, and required in all professions. It is especially important in legal, and law enforcements decisions, where citizens lives are either justly, or unjustly affected. Therefore, whichever path the lives of those who profess love for God takes them, career-wise, or professionally, they share the responsibility of trusting God as they walk by faith. This trust calls believers to spiritual commitment, and dedication to God's word, God's purpose, and God's callings. God calls His disciples to follow Him, and learn from Him. Before any spiritual assignments are given, God prepares followers for success.

God calls leaders to positions of leadership, and authority. He calls the lost, to be saved. He calls the weak to become strong. He calls light out of darkness. He calls love to overshadow hate. He calls for justice, and "judgment to run down as waters, and righteousness as a mighty stream," (Amos 5:24, KJV). The legal system, in America is not always thought to be fair. Often, the judgement given to lawbreakers are not based on the crime, as much as the color, or socioeconomic status of the person(s) accused. The perceived unbalanced scales of justice tend to imprison the poor, the minorities, and those lacking sufficient financial resources to effectively defend themselves with highly qualified attorneys. In cases where justice become political tools in the hands of ambitious people vying for positions, promotions, or status, the law will often yield unjust decisions. People lose their freedoms, and they become nothing more than usable objects, or steppingstones.

There is the need for a spiritually qualified legal system that practice law and order in the manner which ensures equal justice for all. It is the kind of justice of which the Prophet Amos' repentant message to the people of God spoke to concerning them following after idol gods. He told them that God was not moved by their religious practices, their sacrificial offerings, nor their songs of praise as long as justice was not the priority of their worship, praise, and living (Amos 5:21-24). The Prophet Amos was sent by God to the people of Israel with the message of repentance. His emphasized spiritual message to them was on the subject of justice because the people of God had strayed away from the spiritual principles of fairness, fair treatment, love for God, and had forgotten that they were forbidden to have other gods before Him (Exodus 20:1-5, KJV).

Justice is defined as the quality of being just. Simply stated, it is the aspect of treating everyone fair. It is putting into practice that which we have come to know as the Golden Rule: "Do unto others as you will have them do unto you." Jesus said, "Thou shalt love the Lord thy God with all thy heart, and with all thy soul, and with all thy strength, and with all thy mind; and thy neighbor as thyself," (Luke 10:27, KJV). Justice is both a spiritual assessment, and a spiritual judgment. It is about doing right in the sight of God.

CHAPTER 21

Wounded by Church Hurt

It is said, by some people, that when it comes to being hurt by other people, there is no hurt like church hurt. I guess what makes this sting so painful, to those injured, is that most people believe the church to be God's house of safety, love, kindness, respect, and support. This assumption causes vulnerable people to let down their protective defenses. When the hurt occurs, it often leads to long-lasting negative results. Some hurt people leave the church, and come back after long periods of absences. Others hurt people leave, and never return. For those that give up, or have given up on the church, their decisions usually are based on the remembered stings, and pains they received from some church members. Perhaps it was some people that sang in the choirs, or those praying at the altar, and even possibly the preacher in the pulpit. This kind of hurt has been considered by many people injured, too painful to be repeated. They decided to give up on church, and convinced themselves to never attend church again. They don't trust not being hurt again.

There was a man I knew, a long time ago, who experienced church hurt. It adversely affected his spiritual life, and his church association. He was just an ordinary man who liked singing in the choir. He was not the kind of church member that sought any positions in church. For the most part, church for him was a Sunday service where people came together, sang, prayed, preached, and went home. Like many men in his time, and community, he gave God his time (Sunday morning worship), and rest of the day belonged to him. He was a loving man, and a lovable person to know. He liked to make people happy, make them laugh, make them feel good about themselves. Because of his mannerisms, and his efforts to be pleasing to others, people gave him the nickname, "Good Time Charlie." Although he liked to party, and have fun, he was a good family man. He and his wife had eight children. He was not one that got involved in many church activities, but he supported and encouraged his children's participation in the teaching and training activities of the church.

The church hurt he experienced was a great spiritual tragedy. One that could have been avoided. The church event that triggered this calamity was the annual men's day celebration. As with most church programs at that time, the focus was on fundraising. The format used was that of assigning all the men in the church to small groups, and choosing one man in each group to be captain over the group. This format had been successfully used before. Instead of using the same people each year, new names were placed at the top of the teams. The chairman of the committee, along with other men of the church, thought that making Good Time Charlie a captain would be a good thing. It could build up his interest for doing more church works. Although, Good Time Charlie wasn't too comfortable with this selection, and not fully aware of what he was to do, he went along with being named captain. Perhaps others put their arms around him, or on his shoulders, or even patted him on the back with the encouraging words, "You can do it." Not willing to let them down, he went along with the suggestions.

The responsibility of the captains was to ensure that all the men on their lists raised the required amount of money for the occasion. Additionally, the process was made competitive in that the captain with the most money would be recognized, and honored. What happened to Good Time Charlie was wrong on many accounts. His situation should become a footnote on how to not select people for church leadership, and/or fill vacant church positions. When it comes to church positions, people first of all should be willing to serve, not coerced. If selected for specified tasks, the selection should be according to their gifts, talents, abilities, and interests. Such descriptions for leadership, or involvement for this occasion did not fit Good Time Charlie's selection to this leadership position. The intention of the chairman was sincere in his efforts to involve more men in church leadership program by giving them greater opportunities, and responsibilities. However, the consequences for selecting wrong people as leaders were not considered. One criterion, or qualification the committee thought to use for considering new men as captains was the number of years they had been in church, and hadn't been selected (not a good reason for selection). They asked these new men to be captains over teams because they wanted to involve more people and making them leaders will encourage them to give more money (another bad reason). Some thought this was a way to get Good Time Charlie, and other men to become more active in church events (the straw that broke the camel's back). This method of recruitment is doomed for failure every time it is applied. If success is to take place in church activities, programs, events, and especially church leadership, don't ever select anyone just because they are there, or you just need someone. That is if you value the position, and the outcome. Do not select an inactive church person to do active church work. They have already demonstrated their unwillingness to be active. You don't give church work to be done by people that either don't come, or occasionally come to church. Let's follow the model, and guide Jesus applied when selecting people to lead, guide, and participate in the church, and/or the spiritual works of God.

Jesus' ministry team selection consisted of men who were working. He asked them to follow Him. He did not choose idle men, nor lazy men, nor men who worked part-time. He chose men who were diligent workers. Men who were determined, and willing to do the assigned work (Matthew 4:18-19). After selections of these men, Jesus didn't try to rearrange their gifts, talents, knowledge, or abilities to make them conform to some idealized holy images. Rather, He trained them along the lines of who they were. For example, Peter, Andrew, James and John were fishermen. That's what they knew. That's what they did. Jesus modified the focus of their practiced trade by teaching them to apply their skills used for catching fish, to catch men. Matthew was a tax collector. His strength was in monetary assessments, and collecting of taxes from the people. His worth in the ministry of Jesus became a strength after he was taught to use his gifts, and skills of resource assessments to meet the spiritual needs of the people. Judas, who betrayed Jesus, in spite of his actions, brought some positives to the ministry team. His background associations had instilled in him a strong aggressive nature, and mindset. He was anxious to get things done. Although this attitude, and approach caused his downfall in relation to waiting on Jesus, and not getting ahead of Him, his energy to get things done is what every ministry needs. However, energy for spiritual works must always be seasoned with God's timing, and our willingness to wait on the Lord. "But they that wait upon the Lord shall renew their strength; they shall mount up with wings as eagles; they shall run, and not be weary; and they shall walk, and not faint," (Isaiah 40:31, KJV).

Well, back to church hurt. Remember Good Time Charlie? Leading organizations was not his strength. Serving as a team leader was not his calling. Fundraising, and guiding his team to set, pursue, and reach goals were not within his skills-level. He didn't know how to do it. He had questions without sufficient answers. Such questions as, who could he ask? What would they say? What would they think of him as a man? So, he didn't ask anyone. The day came for captains to make their reports. Most of the captains brought positive reports of attaining their financial goals, and gave it to the Chairman. However, Brother Good Time Charlie was hesitant to make his report because it wasn't as complete as other captains' reports. Nevertheless, he had done his best. When the Chairman looked at the report, he noticed that Good Time Charlie had paid less than the people on his team. The Chairman in a rude, and degrading tone spoke to him about his shortcomings. It didn't sound like a man-to-man interaction to Good Time Charlie. He was made to feel like it was an adult-to-child reprimand. The Chairman asked him how could he as the captain let his team members do better than he did? Feeling embarrassed, and made to feel ashamed, Good Time Charlie offered not a word of explanation, nor any words at all. He simply laid the money on the table, walked out of the church, and never went back. The Chairman never knew that the money Good Time Charlie paid came out of his own pockets. He was not a salesman. He didn't know how to ask, or beg for money. He was not a man of wealth by any means. He represented the best way he could. He gave what he had. The blame, if that is an appropriate claim for this mishap, rests solely on the Chairman's shoulders. Perhaps they all should have known that this ill-conceived intention was not the best, or most effective method for getting more people involved in church works. The Bible warns about giving novices duties before they are prepared for such responsibilities (I Timothy 3:6, KJV). Good Time Charlie was not a novice church member. He was a novice in fundraising. He was a novice leader, and novice as captain of a fundraising team.

In 1981, this loving man died. It was his motivation, and aim in life to bring joy to all that he encountered. Where is the justice in this, you may say! Well, it was not in the unwinnable position this man was placed. Walking with God, and finding spiritual justice mean looking beyond what is seen to grasp and understand that which is not seen. The Apostle Paul wrote to the church in Corinth, "While we look not at the things that are seen, but at the things which are not seen, for the things which are seen are temporal, but the things which are not seen are eternal," (II Corinthians 4:18, KJV). Because God looks at the hearts of men, at the day of judgment, I believe that God will say to this loving, and lovable man called *Good Time Charlie,* "Well done." The gift he gave was from his heart. His giving to that men's day program was his best. Perhaps his contributions that day could be equated to what Jesus observed of a widow woman, who in giving at the temple, while many others gave in abundance, gave only two mites. Nevertheless, Jesus declared that this woman gave more than others, (Mark 12:41-44, KJV). How could this be? When is less greater than more? Jesus looks into the hearts of people.

This woman gave what she had. She gave her best. She gave from her heart. Good Time Charlie did not give as much as other captains. He gave what he had. However, his profession of faith revealed that he knew God personally. His willingness to encourage others, and bring laughter into their lives was a spirit of kindness that glorified God. Although, he never went back to that church building, he maintained a true faith in God. The songs of the church remained in his heart. Quite often he would start singing whether he was around church people or not. He was no longer an active church member, but from his heart, he still walked with God.

CHAPTER 22

Seeking Justice in An Unjust System

T he main entrance to the United States Supreme Court building is on the west side facing the United States Capitol. On either side of the main steps are seated marble figures. On the left is a female figure, *the Contemplation of justice* (the action of looking thoughtfully at something for a long time). On the right is a male figure, *the Guardian, or Authority of Law* (legal authority to care for the personal, and property interests of another person). Above the entrance of the Court is inscribed the words, *Equal Justice Under Law.* This building serves as the equalizer of lawmaking, and citizens' assurances for justice, safety, and security under the law. The U. S. Supreme Court is the third branch of governmental operations in America. Its primary responsibility is to ensure that laws passed, and enacted throughout the country, do not violate rights of citizens. That laws passed are just, fair, and constitutional. Throughout its history, the U. S. Supreme Court has been pivotal in shaping America's cultures, and societies as it expanded from being a White's only domination authority to the inclusion of other races as citizens of this great land. You see, America is a composite nation consisting of citizens from across the globe that migrated to this land to call it their home. President John F. Kennedy, the 35th president of the United States, declared years ago that *America is a nation of immigrants.*

Words in the national anthem states that America is the land of the free, and home of the brave. However, there are times, and voluminous incidents where it seemed that this part of the national anthem do not apply to minorities, including black, and brown citizens. Injustices have been heaped upon them through laws passed by segregationists wanting to keep separation between races, the established way to live. Neighborhoods, schools, restaurants, dining places, stores, water fountains, movie theaters, and even churches, under these laws, were structured for "separate, but equal" ways of living.

Separate, but equal was a legal doctrine in U.S. Constitutional laws which allowed segregationists validation to institute these separatist practices without legally violating the 14th Amendment to the Constitution. This Amendment was established law with the applied purpose of assuring all citizens "equal protection" under the law. The Supreme Court case of *Plessy v Ferguson* (1896) confirmed this practice of separate but equal. It was later determined to be inadequate in providing true equality among the races through separation. Nevertheless, the process of overturning segregation laws, and practices would take a long time to achieve. This slow-to-achieve application of equality for all citizens began with such legal challenges as the 1954 Supreme Court case of *Brown v the Board of Education of Topeka, Kansas.* Followed by the *Civil Rights Act of* 1964 where the U.S. Supreme Court ruled that separate but equal was unconstitutional.

Freedom for blacks in America has been a great, and difficult struggle claiming the lives of men, and women of all colors for the sake of providing citizens their constitutional rights, privileges, and due justice under the law. The road to freedom has always included walking with God. The voices of the oppressed, downtrodden, abused, and outcasts have always been sounded through the church, the oracle of God. Spiritual leaders, men and women, who walked with God prayed out loud for justice to reign. Sang with loud voices songs of hope, faith, and love. They spoke with firmness, and in the authority of God's word. They claimed victory in the faces of threats, anger, beatings, imprisonments, and even deaths. The song, *"We shall overcome,"* often heard, and emphasized among those marching for rights of citizens, sounded a prophetic message of hope. It has been the spiritual expectation, and still reside in the hearts of God-loving, peace seeking citizenry, that one day all of God's children will walk together, stand together, and live together in love. It is the God-kind of love that allowed Jesus, the Savior who came into the world, to set the captives free (Luke 4:18-19, KJV).

CHAPTER 23

We Ought to Obey God Rather Than Men

T he definition of laws in America is basically categorized as being either civil, or criminal. The assessments of crimes committed by lawbreakers are legally determined as to being either misdemeanor, or felony. The violations of these laws are considered to be crimes against the people. The breaking of spiritual laws is crimes against God. There are also religious laws that don't always correlate with spiritual laws. Spiritual laws are sometimes diluted by religious leaders hungering for power. They are used to supersede God's laws through religious creeds, doctrines, and laws for religious organizations' benefits. Such is the case that Jesus' disciples, Peter and John faced as they stood before the Sanhedrin Council, the Jewish religious court, and Annas, the High Priest, on charges of spiritual blasphemy. These charges stemmed from their bold witnessing about the love, faith, and power they had through Jesus Christ. Through faith, in His name, they caused a lame man to walk, (Acts 3:1-9, KJV). This miracle did not go unnoticed by the religious orders. They had seen this beggar sitting at the gates of the temple for years. Unable to explain it away, they tried to ignore what had occurred. The people who witnessed this spiritual happening couldn't stop talking about it. This made the Jewish religious leaders unhappy with Jesus' followers. They made determined efforts to shut down this movement.

The boldness that Peter displayed before the religious council wasn't always his strong standings when it came to his faith, and ability. Remember, it was Peter who stood up in protest when Jesus spoke to them about going to Jerusalem to be tried, found guilty, and crucified. It was after they had observed the Jewish Passover, and shared the Passover meal that Jesus told them that they would all be offended because of Him, and would desert Him (Matthew 26:31, KJV). Peter couldn't believe that he would ever abandon his teacher. Even if all the other disciples did so, he would not (Matthew 26:33, KJV). Jesus brought truth to reality when He told Peter that before the rooster crowed twice, he would three times deny that he even knew Him (Matthew 26:34, KJV). This rebuke by Jesus was hard for Peter to grasp. However, when the synagogue's soldiers arrested Jesus in the Garden of Gethsemane, all the disciples fled in fear for their own safety, leaving Jesus alone (Matthew 26:56b, KJV). As Jesus was moved from courtroom to courtroom, His disciple Peter stood curiously outside by the fire where he kept himself warm from the cold weather. Three times he was asked whether he knew Jesus. Because of his dialect, he was asked whether he was one of Jesus disciples. Each time Peter strongly denied his association with Jesus. When the rooster crowed twice, he remembered the words of Jesus, "Thou shalt deny me thrice," (Matthew 26:34, KJV). In shame, he ran away, and hid himself (Matthew 26:75, KJV). Peter's response to the situation was about his self-preservation. It was about his fear. It was about his arrogance. It was about his spiritual failure.

As Peter and John stood before this same religious authority that condemned Jesus to the cross, they stood without fear for their safety. Although this religious governing body had the power, and authority to physically punish them, or have them placed in prison, they did not waver in either their faith, or commitment to Christ. Knowing the consequences for their stance, they proclaimed Jesus Christ to be Savior of the world. The Council was perplexed by their spiritual resolve, and wondered what they could do to change them. They agreed that Peter and John were simple men, and not scholars, or learners of the law. However, the faith, and strength, along with the words they spoke, caused the council to marvel at their ability to resist their threats, and demands. They concluded that the actions of Peter and John verified that they had been with Jesus (Acts 4:13-15, KJV).

Nevertheless, the Council members believed that something had to be done to interrupt that 'Jesus movement.' After conferring with each other, they threatened Peter and John with severe punishments if they continued to speak, and teach people in Jesus' name (Acts 4:16-18, KJV). The Council's decision to frightened these disciples of Jesus had no impact on them. It was evident that they were willing to endure sufferings for His name-sake. Instead of fear, it was faith from these men of God that empowered them to stand against this religious oppression. It was Peter, the man who three times denied Jesus because he feared for his life, and safety boldly standing. It was Peter, the man after receiving Holy Ghost power, preached on the day of Pentecost where 3,000 souls were saved, boldly standing. This Peter, often portrayed as a man of much sound, but little substance, boldly standing. On this day when Peter and John were forbidden to speak in Jesus' name, Peter spoke with boldness to the Council. "Whether it be right in the sight of God to hearken unto you more than God, judge ye, for we cannot but speak the things which we have seen and heard," (Acts 4:19-20, KJV). This statement of faith sounded so strong that the religious Council had to let them go.

The disciples did not consider their freedom as an opportunity to slow down, or be more cautious in their witnessing, or become hesitant in doing their spiritual works. No, they continued to represent Christ through preaching, and teaching of the word of God. Their persistent faith enabled them to share the gospel message with people searching for a spiritual relationship with God. A closer walk with God. Because their bold actions violated the Council's demands, they were arrested again, and chastised for preaching, and teaching in Jesus' name. In response to the threats of imprisonment, the disciples, the apostles of Christ answered their captors with this affirmation, "We ought to obey God rather than men," (Acts 5:29, KJV).

CHAPTER 24

Setting The Captives Free

Crimes in America have always been a concern for law, and order. Safety, and security as well as for peace, and justice are the focus of law enforcement. Until recent times, adult men, and women were the major violators of the law. However, the current levels of crimes committed often include, alongside adults, growing numbers of young people. Many of them being in their late teens, and early 20s years of age. Why are so many young people finding glamor, and excitement in committing crimes, and doing violence? Could the interests, and association be equated to the images, and influences that smoking, and drinking alcohol had on previous generations? Is it their rite of passage to adulthood? These questions linger with various answers, and some concluding that these are but the actions of this rebellious generation. These young people have no respect for authority. They are an out-of-control generation. They are evil, selfish, and have no consideration for life.

It is easy to label a person, a group of people, or a generation of young people to fit stereotyped images, or predetermined conclusions. It can also create poor self-images in people. Sometimes these negative titles given to people become dangerously affirmed identities that cause them to live out these destructive images. Without effectively addressing the significant issues for dysfunctional behaviors, the same conclusion is reached, labeled, and stereotyped. The social system's focus for resolving these concerns usually limits its approach to problem-solving. Which is okay, except in most cases, problem-solving often turns into a series of problem-searching, and questions with no solutions. Questions such as, what caused these actions, or reactions? Who should be blamed? How many more prisons do we need built? These inflammatory questions become predetermined answers to the exploding problems of crimes, and violence in our communities. Such questions are followed by an evaluating process that often include conducting behavioral surveys, researching families' backgrounds, and using mental illness, or mental instability as rationales for problem-solving. There is too much time sacrificed toward assessing problems when the attention should be focused on spiritual solutions. Problems trouble societies, and communities. Solutions provide opportunities for peace.

Spiritual solutions must be applied to troubled homes, wayward children, and disheartened communities if changes are to occur. Without this spiritual solution actively influencing family living, many of these promising candles will be prevented from becoming bright shining lights. They will remain imprisoned in sin, and their ill-behavioral conducts will lead them down the broad road to destruction. The hope for interrupting these predictable consequences for troubled homes, troubled children, and troubled communities is found in Jesus declared mission stated, 'He came to set the captives free' (Luke 4:18). Freedom, and being set free are liberating words found at the end of peace-seeking journeys. Being set free is to be spiritually delivered, and renewed through Christ Jesus from the power of sin. It breaks the bondage of resistance, and provides clear understanding as how to walk with God through what you see, how you, feel, and your interactions with others. Therefore, followers of Jesus, with voices of praise, testimonial experiences, and powerful witnessing of grace, need to make known this liberating truth. These ambassadors of peace must spread this Agape, or God-kind of love. They through compassionate love give themselves to sharing the Gospel, the Good News of Jesus Christ. It is the Word from God that's filled with love, and kindness. It is life-changing to all lost in a dark world to hear followers of Jesus tell the story of a Savior whose love is so great that it covers a world of sin, to set them free.

Without Christ, sin corrupts the hearts. It causes hateful people to release brutality, inherited hatred, bitterness, and conditioned biases against other people because of color, nationality, religion, or gender. The solution needed for these negatively conditioned hearts is love. The ill-behaviors of people who direct their unlawful, and criminal acts toward others are but symptoms of the sin nature we all share. It is an imprisonment that deepens the cruelty of hearts. It is as a stick of dynamite waiting to explode. Without Christ, it is like being prisoners locked behind bars, or trapped in jail cells.

Prison is a cruel way to live. There are three aspects of prison life I would like to emphasize. The first one is the prison you can see. People being placed in physical prisons run the risk of engaging inhumane, or unjust treatments. We know that prison should be about justice, and not punishment; about penalty, not vengeance; about accountability, and not about being wrongly treated. However, in the natural, there are genuine concerns for prisoners' care, and fair treatment. The second aspect of a life in prison is an unseen concept known as psychological imprisonment which is the mental control of a person, or group of people. Psychological imprisonment is about the manipulation of minds, maneuver of attitudes, and managing behavioral attitudes of others. Many relationships in this psychological imprisonment suffer decline because someone in the relationship wants ultimate control of the other. Psychological imprisonment in marriages eliminates the aspect of partnership, and override elements of love. Respect is reduced to domination, rather than shared devotion between the two. The third aspect is spiritual imprisonment. This aspect focuses on the power of sin, and its depravity to man's soul. All human life that comes into this world are prisoners of sin. Liberation from sin comes through repentance, and reception of Christ as Savior. This imprisonment robs human beings of one of their created purposes for having life, that is the shared spiritual relationship with God. Sin's entrance into God's creation brought with it separation, decay, destruction, and death. Without accepting Jesus, through repentance of heart, sin continues to hold such in spiritual darkness, and imprisonment. Spiritual imprisonment prevents mankind from having loving hearts, peaceful minds, and spirits that renews fellowship with God. Spiritual imprisonment is to be absent from God.

Regardless of which category your entrapment resides, physical, psychological, or spiritual imprisonment, until freedom is achieved, either through pardons, mental liberations, or spiritual deliverance you are yet prisoners. Unless changes occur, things remain the same. If no spiritual changes have yet covered your heart, you can escape your imprisoned state by accepting Christ as your Savior. Jesus came to set the captives free.

CHAPTER 25

Peter Set Free

L ord Acton, a 19th century English historian, is credited for coining the phrase, "Power tends to corrupt, and absolute power corrupts absolutely." Power is usually associated with people in positions of authority whether legal, law enforcements, ecclesiastical, or political. When it comes to the political arena, there are some candidates that are elected to public offices, who initially, have good intentions of acting on their promises to serve, and represent the people. However, after being in office for periods of time, and feeling the power of the position held, some of them lose sight of their priority of representation. Instead of working out of the interests of those they represent, their efforts change to that of gaining power for themselves. Honesty is replaced with shady dealings. Serving all the people is replaced with pleasing the prominent few. The power to change things for the betterment of all is replaced by self-interest, and self- benefits. Therefore, for those reaching this level of personal assessments, it becomes as what Lord Acton said, "Power tends to corrupt, and absolute power corrupts absolutely."

People in law enforcement positions are regarded as first responders. They are there to calm volatile situations, assure safety when troubles surround the community, and treat all people with respect, concern, and proper care. However, when people wearing law enforcement uniforms misuse their authority by talking down to citizens, treating people disrespectfully, or being negative in their relationship with the public, they have forgotten the meaning of duty, and service. When such occurrences happen, it becomes evident that they are more concerned with power than for people. When the badge, and gun have louder voices for dealing with troubling situations, than the heart, and mind of law enforcers, then power, and having control over others are usually the motivating factors. Law enforcement officers must use their powers to defend, and protect the public. They must never permit the authority given to them to become powers that tends to corrupt them absolutely.

The legal system in the United States is designed to afford all that are charged, or who faces charges of violating established laws, effective representation of defense under the law. This legal method of representation safeguards the constitutional rights of citizens to defend themselves by opposing charges levied against them. Such efforts are to seek justice in the courtroom, according to the law. In most courtroom settings, the statue of Lady Justice standing blindfolded, is positioned either outside, or inside the courtroom. This statue symbolizes justice being blind to biases, and partiality. That is, the law imposed on one is the same for another, without favoritism. Judges have the responsibility of ensuring that justice is provided for, and applied to all citizens, without personal biases, based on the law, and the constitution.

Therefore, judges must be cautious in their positions of power to remain mentally alert concerning the law, and the constitution; so as to not abuse the power of judgment entrusted to them. The decisions they render have positive, and negative impact on people lives. This sacred power of the law given to judges, at times are in the hands of corrupt presiders. Corruptions to this well-respected law assessing position are enacted through bias, or self-serving decisions. However, for the integrity of the courts, and the justice system, judges must maintain established laws through constitutional evaluation. They must safeguard the rights of citizens, and fairness to all when executing their offices. Then will justice, and judgment be committed to roll down like waters, and righteousness as a mighty stream (Amos 5:24, KJV).

In the legal field of our government, the office of judges is heralded as positions of prominence. Judges hold great positions of recognition, and honor. Weak-minded jurists will occupy their positions as ways to be known, or establish an identity. When people in legal authority offices lose their perspectives of the position they hold, the duties they are to perform, and the expectations from the people they serve, they lose the people's trust.

Peter was put in prison for speaking the truth about Jesus. King Herod, the Roman governor, in a weak, and spineless move to please the Jewish religious leaders, had Peter, and James placed in captivity. They were judged, and condemned worthy of being put to death for violating religious laws. James, the brother of John was first to face the charges. He was quickly tried, found guilty, and executed. When Herod saw that his decision pleased the people, he took delight in having other followers of Jesus put to death. It was Peter's turn, but because they were in the days of unleavened bread, he was held in prison until after Easter (Acts 12:1-3, KJV). Not only was Peter put in jail, but he was surrounded by armed guards to ensure that he had no way to escape. The religious leaders remembered how they had placed them in jail before to stop them from teaching, and preaching about Jesus, only to find that they had somehow gotten out, and was back in the public square preaching. They were determined not to allow this scenario repeat itself. Therefore, 16 soldiers were assigned to Peter, with two being physically attached to him. Preventing the possibility of escape (Acts 12:4-6, KJV).

What Peter experienced was injustice based on religious differences, power, and greed. He was the victim of religious leaders' fears, doubts, and spiritual ignorance. His projected punishment was beyond rationale for the proposed law violations. Where is justice in an unjust system? Is there no remedy for such evil, and cruelty? What shall we do? Well, as helpless as the situation seemed for the followers of Jesus in providing aid, or deliverance to Peter, they used the only weapon, or method available to them to bring relief, they held a prayer meeting. Paul's encouragement to the church at Rome, in difficult situations, was for them, regardless of the trial, remember that God is still with them. He said that "Where sin abounded, grace did more abound," (Romans 5:20b, KJV). In other words, God's grace is sufficient for every situation.

When the church gathered at the home of Mary, the mother of John Mark, they prayed for Peter. However, they had no idea that they were about to witness the delivering, and liberating power of Jesus. He declared, "The Spirit of the Lord is upon me to preach deliverance to the captives," (Luke

4:18). It was late in the night. The church was still praying for Peter's deliverance. Peter, and the soldiers were asleep. The Angel of the Lord entered the prison. He was a bright light shining in darkness. He touched Peter on the side, and told him to rise up quickly. At His commands, the chains fell off Peter's hands, and feet (Acts 12:6-7, KJV). Peter, through his relationship with God, experienced spiritual deliverance, and his faith in God was rewarded. There are many situations, and circumstances that believers encounter that at times appear leading to defeats. However, faith in God will always make a way for you to succeed, be delivered, and set free. Faith will overcome any, and all negative situations, and circumstances. Trust God, and do not doubt His ability to work things out to your benefits, you will become more than conquerors in Christ Jesus.

Imagine being caught in a situation similar to that of Peter because you declared yourself to be a Christian, and follower of God through Jesus Christ. Would your faith in God cause the chains that binds you to fall off? Well, what if they were not physical chains that need to be broken, or fall off? Would your faith in God deliver you out of your dilemma? Or perhaps you would remain imprisoned under your circumstances because you lacked faith in God to deliver you. The church at Mary's house was praying earnestly for Peter's deliverance. I'm not sure how many of them expected to see Peter walk out of the prison, and knock on their door (Acts 12:12-13, KJV). While they were praying, that's what happened. It was an unbelievable answer to their prayers. We know God can do anything, but would He do that? It was surreal for them. It also challenges us in our prayer lives. Do we really expect God to answer prayers concerning our situations? Why are we surprised when God moves on our behalf? Did we not believe He would? Are we just conditioned to saying that God can do anything but fail without trusting Him for everything we ask, or think? Prayer is the spiritual key needed to open doors of imprisonments.

However, before we become these prayer warriors' judge, jury, and executioners concerning their faith, or lack thereof in the power of prayer, let's remember Peter's expectations. It happened to him. He wasn't sure it was real. When the Angel woke him, broke his chains, and told him to follow Him out of the prison, they went through the first and second wards, and the iron gates that led to the city. Peter didn't know whether it was real, or a dream (Acts 12:8-10, KJV). Perhaps reality awakened him while standing on the porch at Mary's house. Maybe it was when he heard the saints praying for his deliverance. Perhaps it was when he knocked on the wooden door. Perhaps it was seeing the young girl Rhoda, and hearing her call his name. Whatever the conclusion, Peter stood at the door delivered, set free from an injustice waiting to happen.

There is a Peter in all our stories of injustices that need the power of God's word, through faith, and trust in Him for spiritual deliverance. It is easy to build up hate and resentment toward people for how they sometimes treat, or mistreat us. However, if we want judgment, and justice to roll down like waters and righteousness as a mighty stream (Amos 5:24, KJV), then we must embrace Paul's teachings to the church at Ephesus when he cautioned them to not focus on hating people for how they act, or attitudes they display, because the issue is greater than what they do. This is a spiritual warfare. We are on the battlefield for the Lord. Our true enemy is not our neighbors across the tracks. Neither that person on your job, younger than you, who has been made your supervisor, after you trained him/her. It's not that church member who finds faults in everyone, criticizes everything, and opposes all church growth, improvements, and forward movements. No, none of those things rise to the level of spiritual opposition. "For we wrestle not against flesh and blood, but against principalities, against powers, against the rulers of the darkness of this world, against spiritual wickedness in high places," (Ephesians 6:12, KJV).

CHAPTER 26

Stand Up, and Speak Up

Civil rights leader, Dr. Martin Luther King, Jr. said that, "Injustice anywhere is a threat to justice everywhere." He points out that we are interdependent of each other. What affects one will eventually affect us all. He said, "We are caught in an inescapable network of mutuality, tied in a single garment of destiny. Whatever affects one directly, affects all indirectly." Behind this great wisdom quote from a leader who faced unjust charges, who was imprisoned, whose name was scandalized, and was assassinated. He was a man concerned about justice for all. He willingly took a bold stand for America's people, especially the poor. He stood with them, and marched alongside oppressed people fighting against systemic injustices for guaranteed constitutional rights.

During his time of standing against systemic oppression, many in the law, and legal professions used their positions of authority to bully minority citizens through fear and intimidations. Their aim was, and has always been about maintaining power over them. In spite of such efforts, Martin Luther King, Jr. life's works serve as motivation to all citizens seeking justice in America. Resistance is the most effective tactics used to overcome, or stand against systemic bullying. Citizens must stand up for right, speak up for justice, and not let injustices rule the day. Dr. King was a modern-day example of a person willing to stand against social wrongs. His voice was heard as a call to peaceful actions. His speeches addressed rights over wrongs, love over hate, and peace over conflicts. Taking a stance for right causes, right reasons, and for the sake of doing what is right, takes courage. It is the right thing to do. However, far too few people are willing to take this stand. Most people would rather ignore things than getting involved.

Such was the case that I found myself confronted with one day. I was in position to stand up, and speak up for a person that was mistreated. It happened a morning when I was at one of the discounts' stores in my town. The incident involved a woman that I didn't know, and hadn't seen her before; but that's irrelevant. What mattered was my response, or lack thereof. This dear lady had purchased two small heaters from the store the previous day, so she said. According to her, one of the heaters was defective. Each time she plugged it up, it shorted out her electrical circuits. From my observation, the store clerk hearing her complaint had neither empathy, nor concern for the woman's issue. While I shopped, I saw the clerk talking on her phone, to whom I assumed was her manager. She told the person that the woman wanted a refund for the heater. Her laughter during the conversation suggested to me that she, and the person she was speaking with were in agreement about not giving this woman a refund. When she returned to the counter, she, and this woman had more conversation. The woman in disgust decided to leave the store feeling unsupported. She left with her defective heater in hand.

She said to the clerk as she walked out that it was okay the way she was treated. She was going to talk about them, and tell other people about the store. About how she was treated. She left the store.

As I stood there in the line, I thought to myself, "That was poor service. Customer service has greatly declined." A problem was created that could have been, and should have been an easy solution. Just refund her money. If this had been done, it would have been a win-win situation. Instead, it turned out to be confrontational, adversarial, bitter, and disrespectful to the customer. The store clerk was wrong. After the woman left the store, this clerk started calling her the, "B" word out loud. Her words included the statement, that if the customer had said at her counter what she heard her say going out of the door, she would have punched her in the face. Wow!!! Can you believe this? Did they not get the memo about the customer is always right? Did she not care that me, and other customers heard her attitude? I thought about protesting. Leave my items on the counter, and walk out, but I didn't. I knew it was the right thing to do, but I didn't do it. I was frustrated for that lady customer, but I held it in.

Well, it was now my turn to checkout. I quickly found out that I received no better treatment when I stepped up to pay for my items than the woman who discouragingly walked out the door. The other clerk in the store was on her cell phone. I didn't see the phone. It was not in her hands. She had the extensions in her ears. She was talking to some person about last night. She totaled up my items without saying a word to me. Since I was paying with my debit card, she just pointed to the machine, and kept on talking. When I was finished, she just ripped of the receipt, and handed it to me without saying "Thanks," or "I appreciate you coming in," or "We look forward to you coming again." None of that. I was fuming, but it was after the fact. Why did I not speak up when I could have been heard? Was I afraid that I would be rejected, or called some other profaned name? Out of the store door was too late to address the problem.

People lacking the courage, or strength to speak against unjust incidents, like the one I observed, remain by-standers who are unwilling to speak out against injustices. When one citizen, having the ability, and courage to speak up for truth, and righteousness, it makes a difference. Think of what impact a hundred, or a thousand citizens with deliberate courage to speak out would make. Courageous men, and women not willing to tolerate unjust treatments against fellow citizens by anyone, or any system that permits hurt, hindrance, or disrespect in any way to be normalized. These symphonic voices of goodness, standing boldly together for that which is right, will always stop wrongdoings in its place. These wrongdoers will not be given room, agreement, or approval strength, in any way, to hurt, destroy, or defeat the spirit and/or lives of good people they seek to harm. There is a great need for men, and women of God to use their voices of love, peace, and righteousness to address unjust situations. Voices that refuse to remain silent for fear of retaliations of some kind. Rather, they are willing to stand up, and speak up for justice to be done for one, and all.

Dr. King's insight was both visionary, and prophetic, "Injustices anywhere is a threat to justice everywhere." Dr. King didn't possess any special powers, or any unusual abilities greater than his faith, and trust in God. He courageously stood against social, and civil injustices. Dr. King espoused a message of peace. Even when he was unjustly treated, nonviolence was still his method of operation. Although he died a violent death, April 4th, 1968, from an assassin's bullet, his mountaintop message kept his movement going. His cause was right. His battle was for justice. His bold stand for upholding the rights of others were often met with oppositions. Yet, it motivated him to endure criticism, hatred, and even betrayals to allow "Justice to run down like waters, and righteousness, as a mighty stream," (Amos 5:24, KJV).

Dr. King was a Christian leader with a message of love. He led a peaceful, nonviolent movement that challenged unjust systems to live out the American creed. That is ensuring life, liberty, and the pursuit of happiness for all citizens. For his dedication to the cause of justice for all, his love for God, people, and the ultimate sacrifice of his life, America honors this great man. The third Monday in January is recognized as Dr. Martin Luther King, Jr. holiday. On this day, remembrances and tributes are made honoring this fallen leader. He was affectionately reverenced as the "Drum major for justice, drum major for peace." Although we celebrate this day in his honor each year, there are too few people who are willing, or have the courage to follow his example of standing up for justice. Many of these would be leaders today, who speak about civil rights, and moral rights, and constitutional rights, lack courage to ensure these rights. When it comes to law and order, justice, and doing right, many want the glory of leadership, but not the responsibility it requires.

Dr. King, in spite of many personal endangerments he faced throughout his life, did not shy away from the dangers that confronted him. Rather, he continued to speak truth to power. His life became a symbol of hope for men, and women in America. Citizens, who felt suppressed, and oppressed by discriminatory laws, legal rulings, and courts' sentencing that applied more severe punishments to people of color than for whites committing the same, or more severe violations. Dr. King's August 28, 1963 speech, "I have a dream" gave hope to a nation divided along racial, and socioeconomic lines, that one day, America would truly become "One Nation Under God." That it would live out the true meaning of its creed, as Dr. King pointed out, according to U. S. Declaration of Independence, "We hold these truths to be self-evident that all men are created equal, that they are endowed by their creator with certain unalienable rights, that among these are life, liberty, and the pursuit of happiness." Dr. King spoke of a time when black men, and white men, Jews, and Gentiles, Protestants, and Catholics would be able to sit together at the table of brotherhood.

Edmund Burke, 18th Century Irish philosopher, and statesman, is often given credit for the saying, "The only thing necessary for the triumph of evil is for good men to do nothing." Therefore, if justice is to run down like waters, and righteousness like a mighty stream, we must all be willing to stand up for right, and speak up for justice.

FAITH WALKING

PART VII

CHAPTER 27

Going to Church, and Walking with God

I n this 21ˢᵗ Century's immoral permissiveness, the Christian faith is severely challenged by false teachings, religious predators, and religious hate groups camouflaged in pretend love. These challengers are not surprised participants to Christians walking with God. Their influences are recognized for what they are, spiritual disrupters. These influencers are designed to inflict discouragements, resentments, and controversy for people needing spiritual clarity. It is understood by these religious predators that without spiritual understanding of their need for God in their lives, many people will not seek either church, or religious organization memberships. However, because of the teachings, and empowerment of the Holy Spirit, Christians are made aware of Satan's destructive tactics. These pretend influencers have little to no impact on them. The Holy Spirit equips followers of Christ with spiritual armor, and tools to stand against the wiles of the devil, "For we wrestle not against flesh and blood, but against principalities, against powers, against the rulers of the darkness of this world, against spiritual wickedness in high places," (Ephesians 6:12, KJV). The spiritual battlefield is an active warfare engagement for the souls, minds, and spirits of people. Therefore, Christians, in this 21st Century battle of the minds, and hearts of people must emphatically embrace the mission to seek, and save the lost. The time is too urgent to give in to spiritual apathy, and give up.

Going to church has been a weekly activity that many Christians do without thinking. Going to church is what God-fearing people and/or their families believe they should do. Even people who don't consider themselves to be church going folks, pay attention to those going to church, and respect their decisions. Their rationale is simply this, some folks go to church, and some don't. The respect for the church has traditionally been a positive influence on people in the community, and in society. The church is a positive influence on people searching for righteous living, and a right relationship with God. However, there are evil forces in our world determined to create negative views about Christians, and the church. Therefore, church members must ward off spiritual hindrances with applied enthusiasm. The church, through them, must not be portrayed as an out-of-date religious organization that preys on simple-minded, overly superstitious, or other world-minded people. The church must truly be identified as the Body of Christ. The house of God. The house of prayer. The place of refuge. It is where salvation is emphasized.

The Coronavirus pandemic interrupted, for many Christians, the spiritual routine of church-going. Uncertain of the virus capability to infect others, cautions, and precautions for church worship were taken. Adjustments, and accommodations were made through non-traditional mediums, and outlets by churches to provide worship services so their congregations will stay in touch with God. You would think that such is a strange thing to say. Not in this 21st Century, where people have access to religious materials, and technology every day, and twice on Sundays! However, biblical history has recorded times when people become isolated from their worship centers, and regular meeting places of worship, some tend to forget. In our present time, in spite of the engaged restrictions based on the pandemic, through available technology, all who desire to continue participation in worship can do so.

Through the medium of Facebook, Live Streaming, and other outlets, many dedicated church-goers have been able to view church services from the comfort of their homes. During the pandemic, this has been a safe, and cautious way to stay focused on God, and church. However, the word comfort may suggest that when church folks are able to return to in-person worship, many members who have been faithful attenders to church services may find it more convenient to remain Facebook worshippers. This ill-advised substitution does not provide the wholesome fellowship, and worship one gets from in-person participation.

In the time of Moses, it was Egyptian enslavement rather than the worldwide Coronavirus pandemic that caused the people of God this disconnection. The first, and maybe the second generation of the people in captivity paid homage, and devotion to God. However, after a period of isolation, God became a distant reference in the daily lives of the Israelites. When God enlisted Moses into His plan to liberate His people out of slavery, Moses asked God for clarity as to whom he should say authorized this liberation plan. God told Moses to tell the people that "I Am that I Am" sent you (Exodus

3:13-14, KJV). As simple as this identification of God given for Moses to explain who was orchestrating this deliverance from enslavement, the people's distant relationship with God caused them to not recognize Him. It is believed by some people that their faith, and belief in God would be an easy acknowledgement if they either saw, or experienced miraculous things. Unfortunately, this is a false assumption of faith, and belief. True faith is not seeing to believe, but rather believing without seeing.

God demonstrated His power over circumstances through Moses at the Red Sea when the waters divided itself, and allowed the departing Hebrew slaves to walk through on dry land. Unlike the Hebrews, that was granted this miracle at the sea, the Egyptian army that pursued God's people, drown in the Red Sea (Exodus 14:21-28, KJV). Surely this miracle produced faith in God! Or did it? Remember how God presented Himself as a provider, even in desert settings, by raining down manna (bread), and quails (meat) from heaven for His people? Surely, this developed faith in God's people! Or did it? (Exodus 16:12, KJV). In spite of the great number of incidents along their journey toward the promised land, many of the transitioning slaves remained theoretically chained to Egypt. They refused to embrace the God of Abraham, Isaac, and Jacob. Instead, they decided to make their own god, of gold, and silver to lead them back to Egypt's imprisonment (Exodus 32:1-4, KJV).

Church members today must not emulate the mindset of these people that had the opportunity to change their direction from backwards to forward, their thinking from being limited, to unlimited possibilities, and their worship of gods made with hands, to the worship the true, and living

God. The opportunity is now for the church to speak with voluminous voices that will address, and meet the challenges confronting people today. The church is relevant to the times, our time. It remains a hope for spiritual directions. The church is the beacon. A light of hope shining in lives of people, communities, and the world.

CHAPTER 28

A Changed Man

The faith of believers, and the spirits of Saints that have gone to their rest ahead of us, are ever present with us. Although their lives have ended in this earthly realm, their impacts, contributions, and their works still speak for them. According to the writer of Hebrews, "We also are compassed about with a great cloud of witnesses …" (Hebrews 12:1a, KJV). These witnesses of God are spiritual giants whose lives have become pavements of faith, and faithfulness that others may use to develop their closer walk with God. When history will have recorded the lives, and achievements of these spiritual warriors that have gone from labor to reward, much information gathered will identify them as having been ordinary people who loved God. Loving God is an easy phrase or statement to make, but the truth is known by the walk they took, and the steps they made. I am not saying, suggesting, or concluding that this list of spiritual honors do not include prominent, famous, or any other persons of significant stature, or notoriety. I am simply highlighting ordinary saints who fell in love with God.

Deacon Freddie B. Allen, Jr. was such a person to reference. He passed away a few days ago. It was a sad day for his family, naturally, but that sadness also belonged to the church. You see, he was a man who genuinely loved God, his pastor, and especially the church. Years ago, his mindset, and lifestyle was worldly. He was a party man. He was associated with the church, but the church was not so much in his life. His early years fitted into the period of time when many people respected God, and the church, but had limited involvement with either one. I don't mean to infer that people at that time was playing with God in any way. It's just that church participation was pretty much a Sunday activity for most people. It seemed as though that mostly those people labeled as Holier-than-Thou, or coined to be sanctified folks were the ones totally committed to church participations beyond Sunday services. Brother Freddie was quite popular in his early days. His stature afforded him such. He was tall, handsome, and friendly. These physical ingredients he possessed made him a magnet of attraction.

As time moved forward, life for him took on greater dimensions of purpose. The bright lights, and glimmer lifestyle he found himself living left him with a void that nothing he was doing could fill. This sense of needed purpose, and fulfillment in his life, took him back to his spiritual roots in the church. I don't know exactly when things changed for him. I do know that somewhere along the way Freddie B. Allen, Jr. became a changed man. I don't mean change from a sinner to a saint, that happened for him in his youth. He accepted Jesus Christ as his Lord and Savior as a young man. He was baptized, and became an official member of his church. Nor do I mean changed from being worldly, because the church was within him, just distracted by things of the world. I am saying that his heart for the church changed. He came to himself, and recognized the important role the church plays in touching people, and changing lives. With, and through this change awareness of the need for the church came the readjustment of his life purpose, and meaning. This change was both in his natural lifestyle, and in his quest for spiritual fulfillment. He fell in love with God, and the church all over again. In spite of some disappointments, he found among some church members, and leaders in his early church years that caused him to walk away from the church, later in life he found renewed passion for God, and the church as a changed man.

Having fallen in love with God, again, Brother Freddie was in search of a church where he felt God wanted him. Although, he knew people in various churches, and even had family members in several churches in the area, he wanted God to direct his steps. Eventually, he found himself at Tabernacle Missionary Baptist Church, Tuscaloosa, Alabama where Reverend Charles Moore was pastor at that time. Unsure initially that this was the right place for him, he attended services several times there before any commitment to membership was considered. After a period of visits, he joined Tabernacle. Let me make this point, he joined Tabernacle. He didn't join because of the pastor, choirs, or promised positions. He believed that this was the place of worship God wanted him to be. Proof of this commitment came when the church had a major dispute which caused the church to literally split in halves. Half leaving the church, and the other half staying. When he was confronted with the choice of leaving, or staying with the church, Brother Allen made it clear that he didn't join a pastor, he joined the church. That's where he was going to stay.

From the moment he became a member of Tabernacle, his service to God, and church was without questions. He served in various ministry departments, including music, singing in the male choir, and the Spiritual Chorus. However, working with young people, especially boys, and young men of the church became his passion. In addition to working as a youth director, he focused his attention on being a counselor for the boys' ministry group named Crusaders. This youth ministry group was designed to grow, develop, and enhance young men of the church in their knowledge of the Bible, and their spiritual relationship with God. The Crusaders are a designated group under the missionary auxiliary ministry of the National Baptist Convention, USA, Inc. They are trained in several categories to compete at four different levels: local district, wing district, state convention, and national convention. The categories included are oratory, spelling, debates, arts, and Bible drills. His love for these young men was evident as he worked diligently with them, and prepared them for the competitions. His efforts paid off. They began winning competitions everywhere they attended. However, God had other works for him at the church which took time away from working with these Crusaders. He found two outstanding young men, who happened to be twins named Frederick, and Roderick Jones, that he trained to take his place. What an excellent decision, and choice on his part because these new Crusaders' counselors took their assignments seriously. Through their teaching, guidance, and dedicated services, the Crusaders of Tabernacle Missionary Baptist Church, Tuscaloosa, Alabama became the best trained, most competitive, and most productive youth group in the state of Alabama. They won numerous trophies in multiple years at the Alabama state level and below. It was Brother Allen's initiatives, dedication, and commitment to the church that afforded these young men the quality spiritual attention they received.

When the church needed additional Lay leadership, Brother Freddie Allen was one of four men ordained to be deacons with the responsibility of supporting the pastor, and ministering to the needs of the congregation. Deacon Allen was a strong supporter of the ministry. He accompanied the pastor visiting the sick at their homes, and in the hospitals. He became involved in both the local jail ministry, and prison ministry through a program known as Kairos. He took delight in bringing the liberating message of the Word of God to inmates desperately in need of spiritual encouragement. He never did these works for any glory to himself. He did it all for the love of God who lived in his heart.

Deacon Allen was a man of prayer. He believed in the power of prayer. He prayed fervently for the needs of the people, and the church. People of the church often joked with him about his long prayers. Nevertheless, everyone respected him for his genuine care, and consistent willingness to pray. As time passed, many changes occurred in the church that affected the leadership positions. Some of the senior deacons experienced serious health issues, one dear brother suddenly passed away, and the chairman of deacons accepted his call to the preaching ministry. The church needed new leaders of this significant ministry office. Although Deacon Allen, based on his commitment to the church, and his leadership experiences was the logical choice for the chairman position, did not assume the position was his. Rather, he was asked to consider the position. After much prayer, and in support of the pastor, he became chairman of deacons. Deacon Allen was gifted with a beautiful baritone voice that he used to sing to the glory of God. Being missionary-minded and always willing to serve the Lord, and the church, he was often heard singing in the church choirs, "I'll go, if I have to go by myself." "I Am a Living Testimony." These songs are reflections, and indications of the depth of love Deacon Allen had for God. They expressed his appreciation for God having made him to become a changed man.

Deacon Allen's commitment to the office of deacon resembled the biblical deacon Stephen who was one of seven men chosen to serve the people of God (Acts 6:1-6). Dr. Luke, the writer of the book of Acts, described Stephen as a changed man who loved God. This too was evident as Stephen was known for being "Full of faith and power, did great wonders and miracles among the people," (Acts 6:8, KJV). Deacon Allen, as were Stephen, and the six other deacons with him, was appointed to their positions because there was a need for servants. Men who were willing to serve in support of the ministry. Stephen, and the first deacons of the Christian church were responsible for distributing the contributions brought to the apostles by members of this new movement called "This Way." Stephen was effective in his works. He was also on-fire in his witness, and testimony of his love relationship with God. He spoke boldly of his faith in Christ Jesus, even when faced with opposition, and persecution. Until death, he was a strong witness for the Lord. Deacon Allen, also, was known for his strong testimony about God, and how it made him a changed man. Stephen was stoned to death. He died professing the love of God in his heart by asking God "In a loud voice, Lord, lay not this sin to their charge," (Acts 7:60, KJV). Deacon Allen died a quiet death with his family members at his bedside. He, by his faith in God, fought a ferocious battle against several things that had inhibited his health, and limited his ability to do what he loved doing best, serving God. He is gone from us now, but he lives on with us in many ways. His imprints on us as a church family will serve as an eternal reminder of who he was with us. We will remember him as a man who loved God, served God, and lived for God as a changed man.

CHAPTER 29

Why Walking with God Is Necessary

S ome church folks, at times, think that church talk is a language understood by everyone. Such phrases as, Hallelujah! Praise the Lord! Thank you, Jesus! Born again! and Spiritual growth! All are adoration expressions to God that avid church-goers know what is being said. They get the message. However, for many people not acquainted with church rituals, they might not get it. They may not know what such expressions mean. For some of these people, the Bible is just another book; and Christians are folks that always find faults with other people. For such reasons, walking with God needs to be a clearly defined understanding of Christianity; what it means to have a personal relationship with God.

Walking with God is the spiritual relationship affirmed through the process of repentance, renewal, and reconnection through Jesus Christ. Repentance, the first step, leads to forgiveness. Forgiveness is seeking from God a pardon from sin's penalty. Jesus, God's sacrificial lamb, paid the price for sin. He died for the world, so that all through repentance may live.

"Therefore, if any man be in Christ, he is a new creature: old things are passed away, behold, all things are become new," (II Corinthians 5:17, KJV). Renewal reconnects man with God. Through this connection God lives in the hearts of believers.

Walking with God allows Him to teach, grow, and spiritually develop our lives. Walking with God is not an outside show, but an inside the heart dependence on Him. The traditional church hymn, "In The Garden" is a song about partnership relationship. "And He walks with me, and He talks with me, and He tells me I am His own. And the joy we share as were tarry there, none other has ever known." In this born-again relationship, each person is given spiritual duties, responsibilities, and a spiritual identity.

The world remains God's creation placed under the care of mankind. It is a world, at times, conflicted with anger, danger, destruction, and death. However, love remains a powerful countering force against the negatives in this world. Love provides hope, and expectations. Although conflicts are present at all levels of life, the world is still under God's control. The world continues to be a place where faith in God secures unlimited possibilities. It was man's disobedience which caused sin to enter the world. Sin eroded the spiritual life between mankind, and God. It destroyed the peace enjoyed in the fellowship. Sin erected spiritual barriers that fallen mankind could not get over by ourselves. Sin caused the first man and woman their beautiful paradise garden home. Sin cost their lives.

In spite of their disobedience, God's unconditional love was there to clothe their nakedness. His love preserved them to live in a fallen world filled with dangerous consequences.

Through the centuries, times, and years, mankind has continued disobeying God, ignoring God, and turning away from God. There have been some who followed idol gods. Others have built their own gods. Nevertheless, in spite of the many self-serving devised schemes, mankind employed, God has never abandoned us. God's love! His unconditional love continues to provide opportunities for repentance, and restoration. All who receive God's restorative love become spiritually changed with recognized purposes for living.

Why walking with God is necessary? The roads in life are rugged, treacherous, dangerous, and challenging. Walking with God strengthen travelers' ability to make a positive spiritual difference in the world. Without God's presence, Christians are unable to reach people, and spiritually influence their lives. Life is too short, too significant, and too important for Christians to possess, develop, or maintain attitudes of indifference. The needs of a society operating in spiritual darkness is to have motivated, God-fearing, God-loving, Holy Ghost developing Christians whose lives shine brighter. The Apostle Paul wrote to the Corinthian church this mission message, "For God, who commanded the light to shine out of darkness, hath shined in our hearts, to give the light of the knowledge of the glory of God in the face of Jesus Christ," (II Corinthians 4:6, KJV). Walking with God provides the world hope, and faith that rest on this spiritual principle, God is the way to truth, and life. Jesus declared, "I am the way, the truth, and the life. No man cometh unto the Father, except by me," (John 14:6, KJV). Walking with God through Jesus allows us to know God's way, God's truth, and God's life.

God's Way is found in obedience. His will for us is to follow Him. Although we are not robotic to the point that our every move, thought, or action is controlled, or predetermined by God, He has not left us without clear instructions that guides us to righteousness. The references to the two roads in life that Jesus spoke of in the Sermon on the Mount explains more clearly what is meant by God's way. According to the text, Jesus speaking about the Kingdom of Heaven said, "Enter ye in at the strait gate: for wide is the gate, and broad is the way, that leadeth to destruction, and many there be which go in thereat: Because strait is the gate, and narrow is the way, which leadeth unto life, and few there be that find it," (Matthew 7:13-14, KJV).

Two paths: God's way, and the way to worldliness. The broad road leads to destruction. Travelers on this road willingly disobey God's Word, will, and purpose. For these broad-road wanderers, life is about pleasure, power, and personal satisfaction. There is little room for God in their lives. People living on this broad street can see, and know the destructive ends of engaging vices, including drugs, alcohol, smoking, and sexual activities, and still find pleasure in doing them. The enticing lure of the broad street is centered on selfishness, disobedience, and determined efforts to be captains of their own fate.

God's Truth is His Word spoken, written on tablets, and in the hearts of believers. It is the creative power of God's love. John, the beloved disciple of Jesus described God's truth this way, "And the Word was made flesh, and dwelt among us, and we beheld his glory, the glory as of the only begotten of the Father, full of grace and truth," (John 1:14, KJV). God's truth has the liberating power to spiritually enhance all who walk with God. Jesus said, "If you continue in my word, then ye are my disciples indeed: and ye shall know the truth, and the truth shall make you free," (John 8:31-32, KJV). Truth is a difficult thing for most people. We as a society have been conditioned to dance around the truth at convenient times, and avoid it when beneficial to do so.

Truth should never be practiced as an arbitrary tool. It must not be perceived as a "sometimes" principle. Sometimes it is, and sometimes it is not. Truth must always be truth. One of the most recognized lines regarding truth is heard in the movie, "A Few Good Men." Actors Tom Cruise, and Jack Nicholson portrayed characters in a courtroom confrontation. While being interrogated on the witness stand by the attorney (Tom Cruise character), who demanded the truth from this witness, (Jack Nicholson character) shouted, "You can't handle the truth!" Truth is difficult to handle for those motivated to avoid doing right, or who want to cover up wrongs committed. In such situations, truth is sacrificed for pleasures, personal benefits, or pretend things not found in reality.

Governor Pilate, during his examination of Jesus, who was brought to him for judgment by the religious leaders determined to destroy Him, asked Jesus the question, "What is truth?" (John 18:38a, KJV). This question was initiated by Jesus' statement regarding the reason He came in the world, "To this end was I born, and for this cause came I into the world, that I should bear witness unto the truth. Every one that is of the truth heareth my voice," (John 18:37, KJV).

God's Life was breath flowed into the spirit of man after being created from the dust of the earth. John wrote of life this way, "In him was life, and the life was the light of men," (John 1:4, KJV). God's life is commitment, dedication, and sacrifice. One day a rich young ruler came seeking an answer from Jesus as to what he must do to inherit eternal life. Jesus' answer to him was both loving, and empathetic, as His manner was always. He did not dash cold water on this young man's ill-formed understanding of eternal life. He didn't ridicule him, or call him dumb for thinking that he could inherit eternal life. Instead, Jesus talked to him about keeping God's commandments. Without naming them all, Jesus asked him about the commandments dealing with man-to-man relationships (which are considered to be horizontal commandments) Do not commit adultery. Do not kill. Do not steal. Do not bear false witness. Defraud not. Honor thy father and mother, (Mark 10:19, KJV). After hearing these commandments, the young ruler declared that he had kept them his whole life. When Jesus told him that he lacked one thing, he was silent because he was told to sell everything he owned, and give it to the poor. This request was based on the vertical commandments (God-to-man relationship). The first one, "Thou shalt have no other gods before me," (Exodus 20:3, KJV). He sadly walked away because he had great riches, (Mark 10:21-22, KJV).

As difficult as it was for the young ruler to understand why he had to give up so much to follow Jesus, it was equally baffling for the disciples who were questioning their benefits for following Jesus. Jesus assured them that such sacrifice was not without rewards. "This I say unto you, there is no man that hath left house, or brethren, or sisters, or father, or mother, or wife, or children, or lands, for my sake and the gospel, but he shall receive a hundredfold now in this time houses, and brethren, and sisters, and mothers, and children, and lands, with persecutions, and in the world to come eternal life," (Mark 10:29-30, KJV).

The life of Jesus is a lively, and purposeful example of knowing why walking with God is necessary. He came into the world with the purposeful mission of redemption. Knowing that He was to become the sacrificial lamb for the sins of the world, never allowed depression, regrets, or violence, nor the praises, and adulations from men to deter Him from walking with God. Across the sands of Judah, His footprints etched out a map of love, compassion, commitment, and spiritual focus on the mission of redemption.

CHAPTER 30

"Never Locked Up, Just Detained"

These were the words of a man, I will refer to as "Joseph" who was in prison for 20 years, innocent of the crime he was convicted. As with the biblical man Joseph who was falsely accused, convicted, and sentenced to prison, so was this man. It is quite common for people placed in prisons, whether guilty, or innocent, to have, or develop negative attitudes, and personal resentments toward people, the penial system, the justice system, and even God for being in such places. It is unusual for someone claiming innocence to not become negative because of circumstances which placed him/her in prison. At the same time keeping faith in God. A faith, and belief that God will deliver him/her from this imprisonment. The biblical Joseph found himself in prison based on his spiritual integrity. He refused to succumb to the trappings set by a married woman who lusted for his attention, and affection. Her husband had given Joseph authority over everything under his control, except his wife. Joseph honored his position, and respected the man who trusted him. However, the wife had her own agenda. Despite her seductive plans, and devious maneuvers, Joseph refused to give in to her enticements. Feeling the scorn of rejection, this ruler's wife falsely accused Joseph of sexually assaulting her. She used his coat as proof (Genesis 37, KJV). How do you disprove a negative? It is almost impossible to do so when truth is sacrificed for convenience. Joseph was thrown into prison. He was there 20 years with no indications that he would ever see freedom again.

Would it be wrong for Joseph to become bitter because of his imprisonment? Could we blame him if he did? Would the years change his attitude from being positive to that of harnessing negativisms? Could we blame him if he did? Would his faith in God wane, or even dissipate because praying, and prayers seem to be of none effect? Would he feel as though God had abandoned him to the cold dark stench of prison living for doing the right thing? Could we blame him, for feeling this way, if he did? Well, we don't have to blame him for such thoughts, or feelings because the biblical Joseph never gave any indications that the above questions applied to him. Although, they could have been his response. Nevertheless, God, Jehovah Nissi (the Lord my refuge), the God of Abraham, Isaac, and Jacob, is a God of justice and righteousness. He will never forget, nor leave His own. God worked it out for Joseph, through his ability to interpret dreams, to exalt him beyond prison to being second in command of a whole nation. What a mighty God we serve! What was meant for evil God reversed it, and made it good.

This other man referred to as Joseph was not freed from his sentencing. He served all 20 years. It seemed cruel for this innocent man to have had these valuable, and valued years of his life stricken from his possibilities. What could he have been, or done during this time? Twenty years is almost one-

155

third of the biblical life expectancy (Psalm 90:10, KJV). After his life, and career choices interrupted by this prison term, options for career, and finding sufficient employment were greatly reduced. Getting out of prison is often easier than getting over prison for most people seeking a second chance in life. Some people never let former inmates get over the stigma of having been in prison. Their choices are constantly faced with rejections, lack of trust, and negative associations. Innocent, or guilty, the response from an unforgiving society leaves these freed from bondage citizens treated as outcasts. Being a former inmate, there was room for bitterness for this unjust sentence, but not in this Joseph's heart.

During his 20 years in prison, he saw inmates convicted of murders set free, or were granted parole, but not him. He witnessed other law violators who had committed, and were convicted of extremely serious, and violent crimes, leave prison, and return back into society, but not him. Every time he came up for parole considerations, he was rejected. With every rejection of release came the opportunity for him to become negative, blame others, embrace bitterness, and store up hatred toward any, and all that such accusations would apply. No! That's not how this Joseph responded. After each failure to achieve freedom, and relief from his imprisonment, he went back to his prayer area. Through faith in the God with all power in His hands, he started the process of expectations all over again. There were two basic reasons for his continuous denials. One was ignorance by those who wanted to make him guilty by association. Not for what he actually did, which was nothing. The other reason was the pride lawyers, and judges who were more interested in win, and loss records more than right decisions.

As unfair as this ordeal was for him, this man Joseph maintained his strong faith in God, and a highly contagious positive attitude. This positive approach of his toward the conditions he was placed became an asset for him. He was granted certain privileges, and given positions in the prison that allowed him to spiritually grow, and develop. Although he was in prison, he never considered himself as being locked up, just detained. His rationale was that no one can lock up his mind, his spirit, and his undying faith in God who would deliver him. Joseph! Joseph! Joseph! What separated you, brother from the norm? Was there strength of will planted in your life growing up in a family that loved God, believed God, and always trusted God? Was it your trust in the concept of doing the right thing, knowing that doing right will pay off after a while? Was it simply not giving in to a system designed to break your spirit, and your will? Was it your identity that you protected from accepting the label of being called by other names? Regardless of what applied to your endurance, you deserve applause. You did the time, although you didn't do the crime. Now you live a free man. In spite of having served this impactful time of your life, there was no anger in your voice, no vulgar speech on your tongue, nor any low-rated language coming from your mouth, or on your lips.

He spoke about life, and living optimistically. He treated people with kindness, respect, and he showed love to everyone. This man Joseph differs from the biblical Joseph in the sense that, on his release from prison, he was not placed in high positions in society because he interpreted dreams, but it was his ability to spiritually dream that gave him the hope, capacity, and motivation to make his dream of freedom, a reality. His faith in God delivered him to freedom from detainment. You may say, how could that be deliverance if he did the whole sentence? The answer comes through these observations, and recognitions. He was free. Free from having to report to someone, or some law enforcement agency. He was free from having someone always looking over his shoulders, and checking on him. He was free to move where he wanted to move without having to get some supervisory approval from any law-focused authority figure. He was free to live the life he dared to dream. God delivered him from the negative because he remained positive. God delivered him from the injustices that detained him because his faith caused him to trust a just God. God delivered him to freedom, because that's what Jesus came to do, set the captives free (Luke 4:18, KJV). Because he trusted God, and would not give in to the imprisonment that refrained him, it was his positional thought that he was never locked up, just detained. God bless this man referred to as Joseph.

CHAPTER 31

Conclusion

Why walking with God is necessary for love, happiness, peace, and justice? Walking with God fills the voids of wasted time, lost opportunities, and lack of spiritual fulfillment. Initially, this writing began as an expose on the spiritual, or lack of spiritual relationship many church members have with God. It is our belief that the heart of Christian living, and church work, by its members, is dependent on the passion within them to do it. The focus of the Christian church is to influence sinners to be saved. In order for Christians to spiritually impact this world of darkness, church members must follow Jesus's directive, "Let your light so shine before men, that they may see your good works, and glorify your Father which is in heaven," (Matthew 5:16, KJV). The ways of the world are prompted by destructive obstacles, pitfalls, and challenges structured to stifle enthusiasm, drown excitement, and steal spiritual joy. Walking with God prepares church, and spiritual leaders to their posts of "Perfecting the saints, for the work of the ministry, for the edifying of the body of Christ ...," (Ephesians 4:11, KJV).

The Christian church, with all her flawed members, remain the single-most important institution offered to mankind with the divine purpose of providing hope, life, and spiritual deliverance. Christians are to remain prayerful, and faithful. Christians' enthusiasm for reaching the lost needs to become that sacred fire burning in their hearts.

Come alive church! Come alive! Sing to the glory of God saints! Sing to the glory of God! Stay alert Christian brothers, and sisters! Stay alert! Tell the story with power, love, and authority church! Tell the story! Open the doors to the church saints! Open the doors! Teach, Preach the Word of God Watchmen! Teach, Preach the Word! Stand shouting on the walls Spiritual Leaders! Stand on the walls! Shine for Jesus church! Shine for Jesus!

When the saints go marching into glory on testimonies, and praises of how walking with God enabled them to overcome challenges to their faith; how walking with God prevented many destructive pitfalls, and obstacles purposely designed, by the enemy, to hinder Christians' growth, and spiritual progress; then will be the time for accountability. A time to praise God for His unconditional love. The church will rejoice as being His instrument of hope, and salvation, having been elevated to set on a hill, and seen by all. The Saints will be given voices with new songs of praises. Worshippers will give thanks for the church being the heart of the Christian works. Because of the church, God ordered believers' steps in the pathway of righteousness. He caused their lips to sing praises to the Lamb of God who was nailed to the cross for the sins of the world.

His sacrificial act of love took away the sting of death in sin (I Corinthians 15:56, KJV). He made it possible that all could have eternal life, "Not willing that any should perish, but that all should come to repentance," (II Peter 3:9, KJV).

Hear the conclusion of the whole matter: Walk with God when you seek love, whether it's with a spouse, a friend, family members, or your parents. Let love be your heart expressions for the privilege of sharing your life journey with people you care about, and who cares about you.

Walk with God in your quest for happiness. Let your happiness emote around your spiritual relationship with God. His unconditional love has provided the spiritual foundation for happiness. Happiness is the smile you share, and the joy that comes from your heart. Happiness is the result of being secure in God, and sheltered in His love, protection, and care.

Walk with God for the peace that passes all understanding. Let peace directs your actions, and responses to the various conflicts encountered, knowing that soft answers turn away wraths, bitterness, angers, and vengeances, "A soft answer turneth away wrath: but grievous words stir up anger," (Proverbs 15:1, KJV).

Walk with God for the justice that liberates the soul. Let the presence of God in your life assures victory for you, regardless of what accusations, or false charges are levied against you. The promises of God ensure us, "That all things work together for good to them that love God …," (Romans 8:28, KJV). "Trust God with all with all thine heart, and lean not unto thine own understanding. In all thy ways acknowledge him, and he shall direct thy paths," (Proverbs 3:5-6, KJV).

The church of the living God remains the spiritual hope for a world lost in sin. The mission of the church is to seek, and save those who are lost. Touch lives of sinners with the invitation to come from darkness into God's marvelous light. Remember, the church that Jesus established upon a rock (Matthew 16:18), still set symbolically on a hill. It cannot be hidden. Jesus acknowledged the church to be known as "The house of prayer," (Matthew 21:13, KJV). The Christian faith is the greatest power of influence believers have to lead lost souls to Christ. Therefore, it is urgently essential for Christians to be genuine in their walk with God. To God be the glory!

CHAPTER 32

After Thoughts

Seeing is Not Always Believing

The other day, without intending to do so, I made my seven-year-old grandson Matthew sad when I told him that the magic of magicians was not real. The issue began when he asked why magicians had magic wands. I told him that the wand was used as a distraction because magic is not real. I didn't realize at the moment how sensitive, or insensitive my response sounded to him. To him, magicians and magic were real. When he told me that my answer about magic made him sad because I said that magic was fake, I tried to clear up my assessment of the topic. I told him that I didn't mean that magic was fake. He argued that I said it was not real. I told him that the tricks that the magicians did were real. The skills of the magic trade were real. The performances were real. However, what we see them do are distractions. The distractions are what make the magic work. They are what make the magic real. I wasn't sure whether my explanation about magic, and magicians made a difference to him. He started playing on his tablet, and the discussion went no further that day.

The next day our conversation about magic, and magician continued. This time he took the lead. Instead of allowing his feelings to be the concern, he decided to be creative. He told me that since I said that magic wasn't real, he was going to create a magician character on his I-Pad tablet. Then it would be real. He did it. The subject was closed as to whether magic, or magicians were real. The concept of a magician, and his performances caused my attention to focus on the world of our young people. They are introduced to, and made to accept the conditions that adversely affect their growing-up process. So much of the world's politics is unloaded on them without considerations of whether they may be given too much of life issues way too soon. Without sufficient maturity, mental capability to adequately digest, and dissect its impacts on them, the consequences will unconsciously yield negative results. There is not a day in the life of young people in America today that some other young person's life ends tragically through either violent, criminal, or some other destructive means. Guns are major weapons used to cut short potential lives of many young people. Drugs are another culprit that endangers the potential life-spans of young people. Perhaps the most disturbing of all these categories of dangers is the increased numbers of young people taking their own lives through suicide methods, often associated with bullying, low self-esteem, the fear of being exposed for thinking or believing to be gay, and/or for lacking the will to live.

We could play the blame game, but what good would that do? The issues of concern will remain unresolved. Our children are exposed to serious mental, psychological, and physical dangers that impede their growth, development, and ultimately will cause their demise. Still, too few people are showing concerns, or sounding the alarms. Our children, and young people are becoming as numb to these social woes as the adults supervising them have become. When young delinquents' activities are relegated to the norm, we hear about killings, robberies, young people dying, going to prison, and are neither surprised, nor phased by their occurrences. This attitude of 'Oh well' must not become society's responses to such calamities. Under these conditions, life will not go on for many young people. The saying, 'seeing is believing,' that many older people have said, has been replaced by this generation of young peoples' attitudes that suggests, 'what I see others do won't affect me. I can handle it.' This generation of young people who seems to have lost respect for their elders, authority, and the values of life, need to once again be given purpose, meaning, and personal integrity.

Previous generations, through their rejections, and rebellion against established social norms, eroded the foundation of structural, and spiritual life values that current generations have to contend with, or redefine. The values of society used to be established on such moral platforms as the home, respect for elders, and the church. The home was viewed as sacred shelter, good manners were part of children's training, respect for older adults, and authority figures were the right discipline of practice, the church was with reverence, and the church was God's holy place. Life was thought to be the methodical process of growing up one day at a time.

Therefore, much of what many parents, and society would consider important, and necessary for young people to learn, and discover about life today, for their personal growth, and development, seem meaningless to some of them. This not caring attitude, by vulnerable young people, make them easy prey for charlatans' manipulations. The consequences of lost personal values are devastating. The absence of respect for life will promote senseless killings with young people, all across this great land, dying way too soon. The use, and experimentations with illegal drugs, the glorification of guns, and automatic weapons, are destructive tools that will take away, or destroy too many young lives.

When it comes to the use of illicit drugs, all who engage in this destructive process by either growing it, distributing it, selling it, or personally using it, are doomed to failure. The conclusion is the same for all participants, failure. They will either be caught, arrested, and put in prison, or they will be shot, and killed over the money. Some will rob other users, or potential sellers. Still others will do damage to their own bodies from these drugs, or die from drugs overdoses. In each, and every scenario listed, the end result is the same: negative, destructive, and death. Although these results are available to young people to observe, and assess their worthiness, for many, the flaws don't count, or matter. They still choose to engage themselves in this process, because for them, seeing is not believing. Guns in the hands of juveniles, without proper adult supervision yield colossal destructions.

A false statement of power, and being powerful has been inserted into the thinking of many young people regarding having, and using guns. Instead of fighting with hands, and maybe a light stick, or two to win the battle, today's scrimmages often end with gun-play that leave one dead, and one going to jail. Although the number of young people dying from guns seems to rise each week, the statistics don't deter the interest of other young people from trying to get, and use guns. Deaths, funerals, and gunshot injuries have not stopped these young men's pursuit of this volatile danger. With black, and brown youths being the major ones attracted to this illegal vice, it's not hard to sense, or believe the conspiracy of some that this epidemic in their communities are the negative influences of manipulating outside forces.

This theory may possess some validity as to who is making these instruments of death available to young people in varied minority communities. High-cost munitions, and weaponry made convenient to unemployed young people to acquire, and possess raise suspicions as to who is funding these destructive tools. The power to convince these young victims to engage in their own demise, as well as inflict dangers, and death on families in their communities is the works of manipulating predators, and charlatans. The aim, purpose, and agenda of these perpetrators are selfish, greed, and the thirst to be, or seem powerful. As devious as their ploys may be, and as destructive the damages their recruitment of young people has on the health of communities, the blame, or responsibility for such conditions rest not with them alone. Communities, and parents! Parents, and communities are participants as well to the kind of atmosphere, and environments young people are exposed to, and live in. What is allowed to come into the community affects all people in the community. That is why we must always be conscious of what children see, and are exposed to. Children are impressed by what they see. They become, and/or apply what they see people do to their lives.

That is why it is essential that young people today are given good, solid information about the issues, and values of life. They need comparative knowledge of consequences so as to become right decision-makers.

When Truth is silent, Right has no voice! Parents become children's best friends, not their mentor and guides. Adjustments are required to restore order, control, and the duty of parents to teach their children respect, love, and kindness. Tough love requires parents to establish rules, and consistent discipline that support their children growth, learning, and respect for others. Tough love!

Without aggressive efforts to curtail this current trend for accepted violence, things will become progressively worse. For many young people, it's a mind game that often ends with those engaged not believing what they see. That is why we must not overlook the principal aspects of magic. The magicians find ways to distract targeted audiences' attention so as to make the tricks appear real. Tricks! That's the magic of these predators who come promising one kind of lifestyle to these vulnerable youths, while deflecting the true nature of their involvement with them. Flashing large amounts of money, building up false confidence in their identity, importance, and power, are few of the tools these outside predators use in their magic tricks. They use these tricks to manipulate young people who are unsure of their identities, or purposes in life. Truth must come to the light.

It is in these occasions that the church must speak revelatory truths about consequences of making bad choices, and wrong decisions. To address the real damages being done to generations of young people that we call the future, it must be clear to them so that they will believe what they see, and not be distracted by the wands in magicians' hands. If our children are going to be saved from these destructive methods used on them to thwart their interests in building up rather than tearing down, or their interest in preserving life, rather than ending others' lives, they need to hear heart-felt messages of love, care, and concern from parents, adults, and the communities they live. The church must be the symbol of love for the home, family, and community. God must be the center of our attention. They need to hear the message of God's eternal love. His forgiving Spirit.

Faith in the hearts of Christians must be more than a five-letter word shouted boldly on Sunday mornings, but lack life-impacting sounds throughout the week. Faith must not be limited to an inside motivation, but rather an outer garment of faith worn by Christians as solid witnesses for God. There must be a restoration of spiritual relationships that captures the attention of the young, the empty, and the lost. Their lives must find identity in the values of life which comes through spiritual renewal. Guns, and drugs need no longer be viewed as solutions to any problems, issues, or conflicts that are faced. Belief in God, goodness, and basic decency must challenge the negative choices often made. Faith is not seeing to believe. Faith in God makes clear what is seen. Whosoever will submit him/herself to the truth will see the light. Prayer is essential to our understanding of faith, and our walk with the Lord. Prayer prepares us for the thrust of life's challenges, the will to trust, and the patience to wait for His answer.

Therefore, let us pray fervently for changes to occur. Pray this generation return to God. Pray that the church will invest itself into missionary works that take them into the highways and hedges with the message of love, hope, and reconciliation. Let our prayers not be rehearsed chants. Let our prayers be sincere intercessions for those who walk through, and live in darkness. Pray for the motivation of church members to walk with God. Pray that they not become discouraged when the message of God's love is rejected. Pray that they continue to tell the message of Jesus. Pray that they share the love of God. Pray for communities barraged by fear, violence, and deaths. Pray that they become oasis of peace, love, and safety. Pray that God's word will have lasting positive, life-changing impacts on communities. Pray for societies throughout our nation. Pray with the Apostle Paul this prayer that, "The peace of God which passeth all understanding shall keep your hearts and minds through Christ Jesus," (Philippians 4:7, KJV). Pray for the righteousness that Amos spoke about, "But let judgment run down as waters, and righteousness as a mighty stream," (Amos 5:24, KJV). Pray for the kind of peace that brings unity, "Can two walk together, except they be agreed?" (Amos 2:3, KJV). Pray for God's love to be received in the hearts of all, "God is love, and he that dwelleth in love dwelleth in God, and God in him," (I John 4:16b, KJV). Pray that the message, according to Apostle John, motivates us to love, trust and have faith in God, "For this is the love of God that we keep his commandments, and his commandments are not grievous. For whatsoever is born of God overcometh the world, and this is the victory that overcometh the world, even our faith," (I John 5:3-4, KJV).

Pray as we walk with God! Pray until God provides the answers! Pray! Pray! Pray! Amen! Amen! Amen!

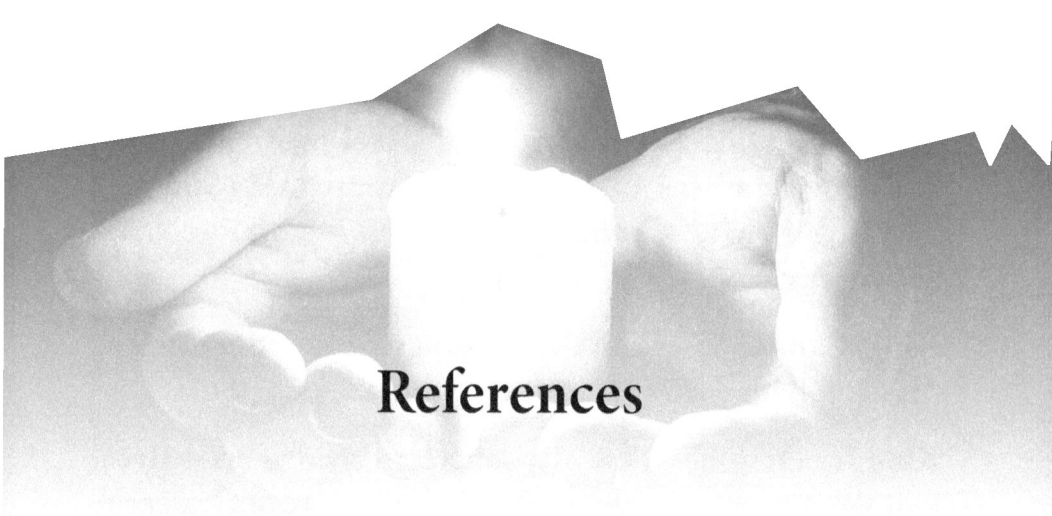

References

Acton, Lord, 19th Century English historian

Bethel Community Outreach Program, Project B.E.T.H.E.L., Tuscaloosa, Alabama

Burke, Edmund, 18th Century Irish philosopher and statesman

Captain & Tennille, "Love Will Keep Us Together"

Cruise, Tom, & Nicholson, Jack, movie, "A Few Good Men"

Devash, Meirav, writer, editor, content strategist and consultant, and beauty & wellness expert.

Frost, Robert, English poet author of "The Road Not Taken." A Group of poems published in *Atlantic Monthly*, August 1915.

Gospel Music Workshop of America Women of Worship Choir (GMWAWOM), "Order My Steps." *Almo Musiccorp,* Notting Hill Music (UK), Ltd. Notting Dale Songs, Inc.

Hemphills, The, Joel Sr., LaBreeska, Joel Jr., Trent, & Candy, Southern Gospel singing group. "He's Still Working on Me," *Capitol CMG Publishing, Universal Publishing Group.*

King, Carole, American singer, songwriter, and musician. "It's Too Late," (1971) Tapestry Album.

King Jr., Dr. Martin Luther, American civil rights activist, and Baptist minister delivered "I Have a Dream," speech in Washington, D.C. (August, 1963).

Melvin, Harold & the Blue Notes, a 1970s soul and R&B vocal group from Philadelphia, Pennsylvania. "If You Don't Know Me by Now."

Thompson, Frank Charles Thompson Chain Reference Bible, King James Version. *B.B. Kirkbride Publisher* (1908, 1917, 1929, 1934, 1957, 1964, 1982, 1988.

The United States Constitution: Preamble to the Constitution

www.ingramcontent.com/pod-product-compliance
Lightning Source LLC
Chambersburg PA
CBHW021630120626
46545CB00002B/476